ME,
THE
MOB,
AND THE
MUSIC

ONE HELLUVA RIDE
WITH TOMMY JAMES
AND THE SHONDELLS

TOMMY JAMES

WITH MARTIN FITZPATRICK

SCRIBNER

New York   London   Toronto   Sydney

SCRIBNER
A Division of Simon & Schuster, Inc.
1230 Avenue of the Americas
New York, NY 10020

First Scribner hardcover edition February 2010

SCRIBNER and design are registered trademarks of The Gale Group, Inc.,
used under license by Simon & Schuster, Inc., the publisher of this work.

For information about special discounts for bulk purchases,
please contact Simon & Schuster Special Sales at 1-866-506-1949
or business@simonandschuster.com.

The Simon & Schuster Speakers Bureau can bring authors to your live event.
For more information or to book an event contact the Simon & Schuster Speakers
Bureau at 1-866-248-3049 or visit our website at www.simonspeakers.com.

Manufactured in the United States of America

10 9 8 7 6 5 4 3 2 1

Library of Congress Control Number: 2009050162

ISBN 978-1-4391-2865-7
ISBN 978-1-4391-4264-6 (ebook)

Insert photo credits: All photos courtesy of the author except photo on p. 4,
top left, courtesy of Karen Grasso, and photo on p. 7, lower left,
courtesy of Carol Ross Durborow.

To my loving wife,
Lynda
—Tommy James

To Kate
—Martin Fitzpatrick

CONTENTS

Prologue — 1

Chapter One: Tuning Up — 5

Chapter Two: Hanky Panky — 39

Chapter Three: Say I Am — 63

Chapter Four: I Think We're Alone Now — 85

Chapter Five: Gettin' Together — 105

Chapter Six: Mony Mony — 133

Chapter Seven: Crimson and Clover — 149

Chapter Eight: Crystal Blue Persuasion — 163

Chapter Nine: Ball of Fire — 183

Chapter Ten: Draggin' the Line — 209

Acknowledgments — 227

ME, THE MOB, AND THE MUSIC

PROLOGUE

Mᵃʸ 21, 1990.

The day began with me rushing off to Chicago to do a concert promoting the release of my new album *Hi-Fi* and the single "Go." It was my first studio album in nearly ten years. I was to meet Ron Alexenburg, the head of Aegis Records, and my manager, Carol Ross, at Newark Airport to catch a flight to Chicago. The band had already gone ahead, and we were all pretty excited about starting the nineties off with a new project. A host of radio stations and press were going to be there. Because Chicago had launched so many of our past successes, it seemed the perfect city to begin our tour. As my wife, Lynda, and I were about to leave, the phone suddenly rang. I was in a rush and kind of annoyed when I answered. It was my accountant, Howard Comart. In a very subdued voice he said, "Morris is asking for you. If you want to see him you'd better get up here right away."

"Oh my God, Howard, I'm dashing out the door to do a show in Chicago. I'll be back first thing tomorrow morning and I'll come right up." There was a pause. Howard said, "Well, okay." But there was a tremor in his voice. I gave him my hotel number in Chicago and told him to keep me posted.

When I got to the airport, I told Ron and Carol the situation, and it cast a shadow over our otherwise joyful morning. The Godfather of the music business, Morris Levy, was dying of cancer. We all had a feeling of disbelief because none of us had ever thought of Morris as anything but invincible. In his sixty-two years, he had created and controlled one of the biggest independent music publishing companies; managed and was partners with the most famous rock and roll disc jockey, Alan Freed; owned the most famous jazz club in history, Birdland; and owned one of the most successful independent record labels of the fifties and sixties, Roulette Records, which also was my record label for eight years.

Morris and I had been exchanging messages through Howard, our mutual accountant, for several weeks, almost like two kids passing notes back and forth in school. I knew he understood how saddened I was by the whole thing and that despite everything, I genuinely cared about him.

When we got off the plane at O'Hare, I was suddenly filled with the old excitement; a sold-out show, in Chicago, to promote a new record. It felt good to feel this again twenty-four years after first signing with Morris and Roulette. Our road manager met us at baggage claim, a limo was waiting outside, and we loaded up and headed for the hotel. The rest of the day went pretty smoothly, the sound check and all the backstage stuff. But all I kept thinking about was Morris. Lynda kept checking our messages at the hotel hourly.

The show went great; the audience went crazy, dancing in the aisles, standing on their seats screaming for more. We played a combination of the hits and the new stuff, but even on stage I was preoccupied. We ended the show with "Mony Mony," like we had done ten thousand times, and did the usual encore. Like always I was hot, sweaty, and out of breath when I came off stage. Carol and Ron met me by the stage door and we all walked back to the dressing room. I had an interview to do with a young radio guy from a local pop station. There was a lot of whooping and hollering around me as I sat down to catch my breath in front of the dressing room mirror. The DJ started asking me questions and I could see the cassette player rolling. The interview had begun. I started off with how great it was to be back in Chicago, then Lynda suddenly came into the room holding a piece of paper. She said, "I'm sorry to interrupt, Tommy, but Morris Levy died."

There was just silence. All day long I had been thinking about what I was going to say to him, and now I'd never get the chance. I'd heard stories of how emaciated he had become and had imagined what I would feel seeing him like that, but it didn't matter now because I would never see him again.

At that point my interviewer said, "Excuse me, Tommy, can I ask you a question?" I nodded and he said, "Who is Morris Levy?"

Wow, who is Morris Levy? I looked at him in astonishment and realized this kid couldn't be more than twenty-one or twenty-two years old.

"How much time do we have?"

"As much time as you want. I came for an in-depth interview."

"Well, you're going to get one. Is that tape recorder still running?"

CHAPTER ONE

Tuning Up

I was born Thomas Gregory to Belle and Joseph Jackson, on April 29, 1947, at Good Samaritan Hospital in Dayton, Ohio. Nothing special, really. Just one of a few million baby boom kids born that year, born on the cusp of a new age.

Dad was in the hotel business, a roustabout who could manage the books, tend the bar, or fire the bellhops. He was five foot eight, quiet, heavyset, and balding. Mom worked as his assistant or sometimes on her own as a legal secretary. She was Dad's opposite: tall, stately, and prematurely gray. She was straight talking, articulate, and would often use a three- or four-syllable word when a good old-fashioned grunt would do. We had one of those mock portraits of two dogs, an Airedale and a boxer, standing next to each other dressed like people. It was a mirror of my mom and dad right down to the tilt of their hats.

We moved to an apartment on La Salle Street in South Bend, Indiana, and that is the first place I really remember. Living in South Bend in the early fifties meant driving a Studebaker (after all, they were made there, and my uncle Don was on the design team), rooting for Notre Dame (when the Fighting Irish were actually mostly Irish), and being brought up Catholic. The neighborhood we lived in was close-knit and blue-collar. I guess you could say we were all upper lower middle class. And whenever I went out to play, there were always hordes of kids. There never seemed to be just one or two. My folks worked hard because they had to in order to get what they wanted out of life, and since I was an only child, most of their world revolved around me. I always got the best they could give me.

As far back as I could remember it was just the four of us. Oh, did I mention music?

Mom used to tell me the only way she could quiet me down as an infant was to turn the radio up. As soon as I heard music, I would stop crying and listen. It seems like I had my ear in a loudspeaker of one kind or another my entire life. In fact, my first concrete memory is of the family radio, a huge Philco console with a mahogany finish that was twice as tall as I was. It had knobs and dials on it as big as doughnuts. But I always managed to boost myself up and tune in my favorite stations. And of course, there was my record player.

Ah yes, my first record player. It was a 78 r.p.m. kiddy model with an old-fashioned diaphragm attached to the tone arm, which acted as a speaker. The thing was virtually indestructible and could have easily doubled as a murder weapon. It had steel needles that looked like carpenter's nails and always seemed to need replacing after every fifth spin.

My record collection was an odd assortment of "Little Golden Records" for kids interspersed with the pop hits of the day I heard on the radio. I had collected everything from Sammy Kaye to Yosemite Sam. My poor folks were forced to listen to an endless loop of "Mona Lisa," "Mule Train," and "The Three Billy Goats Gruff."

In 1951, when I was four years old, my grandfather gave me an official Arthur Godfrey ukulele, complete with an authentic chord-maker attachment so I could sing and play along with my records. The attachment was hooked to the fret board, and by pressing one button or another I could make a particular chord. Eventually my curiosity got the best of me and I started peeking under the chord maker to see how the strings were being manipulated. As soon as I realized how the chords were made, I got rid of the attachment and made my own chords. It was my first big career move.

The radio, my ukulele, record player, and record collection were my cohorts and confidants. Music was already the center of my life.

Later that year, my mother enrolled me for piano lessons at the local conservatory. During my first recital, I was spotted by a modeling agency and asked to model clothing for a U.S. Rubber "Style Show" at the Indiana Country Club in South Bend. They were enacting a *Life* magazine advertisement depicting a typical American family wearing various ensembles of rubber wear. I was to be the kid in the cowboy suit with, of course, rubber boots. I had to walk down a runway and then freeze like a mannequin. The only problem was that it was way past my bedtime. I yawned through the entire show even when I was supposed to be as still as a picture. The audience was in stitches. It was the first time I was on stage, and I loved it.

In 1956, my father took a job managing a small hotel in Monroe, Wisconsin. It was a big move for us, especially since we were required to live in the hotel. For me, it seemed like a nightmare leaving the old neighborhood, my school, and my friends. I even had to give my dog away. None of us knew if this was going to work, but for the sake of moving up in the world we tried it.

We drove to Monroe and pulled up, not too optimistically, in front of the Eugene Hotel. It was a three-story brick building on a corner of the downtown square. When we walked into the lobby, it became clear that the Eugene was not exactly state-of-the-art resort quality. The lobby furniture was badly frayed and worn. There was an antique switchboard with old-fashioned candlestick telephones. We were all a little overwhelmed.

After we settled in, the first thing I did was explore my new home, and the first place that caught my attention was the bar. It was downstairs from the lobby and just off the dining room. I cannot begin to tell you how exciting being alone in a bar is to a nine-year-old. It was like being the only kid in an amusement park. I remember it being dark and cool and having a strange, sweet odor of Coca-Cola and floor wax. When I threw the light switch, I could see a beautiful, long mahogany bar. I loved the glistening bright colors of the half-filled liquor bottles against the mirror. To my right were a pinball machine and a stand-up bowling game played with a metal disk. To my left . . . THE JUKEBOX.

It was a magnificent Wurlitzer from the late forties that played only at 78 r.p.m. and looked like a tiny cathedral. It was dome-shaped and framed with tubes of multicolored fluorescent lights and small tubes of bubbles going up each side. God, I loved it. I did not know at that point what my folks thought of the place, but I was sold.

The first thing I did was examine the titles to see which ones I knew. Like most jukeboxes of the mid-fifties, the titles represented a knock-down, drag-out between two generations. Perry Como's "Hot Diggity" was right beside "Long Tall Sally" by Little Richard. Patti Paige was rubbing elbows with Gene Vincent. "Papa Loves Mambo" was next door to "Heartbreak Hotel." My next major discovery was of equal importance: the reset button and the volume control on the back of the jukebox. I had it made.

Of course I had it made only until the bar opened at four in the afternoon. When the bartender came in to start his shift, one of his first duties soon became turning the volume back down to a human level. This usually increased *his* volume and he could often be heard swearing as far away as the lobby. I guess you could say we had creative differences. Although living in a hotel was a bizarre and dysfunctional arrangement, we all tried to make the best of it.

The town itself was hard to dislike. Monroe was a small town with a provincial feel to it that made it almost like a village. The downtown area had a grassy square with park benches and flowers built around a Victorian-style courthouse, a great ornate structure with rooks and turrets, and a huge clock tower. It was always busy with people crisscrossing on their way to work or to shop at the local stores. The Eugene Hotel sat on the southwest corner of this square and from my bedroom window I had a panoramic view.

My favorite places on the square soon became a soda fountain and hamburger joint called the Old Fashioned and the Monroe Music shop. That was where the older kids hung out and that was where the music was. Even though I was only ten years old, I loved sitting with the teenagers at the Old Fashioned eating French fries with ketchup in the wooden booths carved with hearts and initials. And always in the background, rock and roll.

If you wanted to buy records, Monroe Music was the only game in town. I was in that store at least three times a week, spending my allowance, and watching my stack of 45s grow as fast as I did. I loved vinyl. I still do. All those labels like Dot, RCA, Capitol, Cadence, Mercury, and Roulette had such distinctive patterns and color schemes. As I watched them spin on my turntable, they were like candy to me. I could almost taste them. I memorized all the info found on each record the way some kids memorized the stats on the back of baseball cards.

In September of that year I started fourth grade and was able to make a lot of friends. One Friday afternoon, our teacher, Mrs. Thurber, let us have show and tell, and while other kids brought in jackknifes and rock collections, I brought my ukulele to class and performed "Singing the Blues" by Guy Mitchell. It was the first time I played for anybody other than family, and Mrs. Thurber actually asked me to bring my ukulele every Friday to sing and play for the class.

It was only a week later that Elvis Presley made his first appearance on *The Ed Sullivan Show*. Elvis's performance that Sunday night was the most exciting thing I had ever seen. A light went on in my head. I knew that this was what I wanted to be and this was what I wanted to do. I and a million other kids suddenly found a new career possibility: rock star. And why not?

Later that night as I stood in front of the mirror with my ukulele, I felt as dorky as a kid with short pants and knee-high argyle socks. If I was going to be like Elvis, then something had to change, and two things were obvious. I needed a guitar and big hair. I didn't know if there were any other requirements, but I figured this was a good place to start. I combed my hair into something as close to Elvis's pompadour as I could and hoped time and Brylcreem would do the rest. If I could just find a way to avoid the barbershop. Sure enough, when I went to school the next day, everybody was talking about Elvis. Any kid with enough hair had it greased back high along the sides of his head, and the aroma of Butch Wax permeated the air.

As if on cue, probably because of Elvis's appearance, two guitars appeared for sale in the window of Monroe Music. I could see them from my bedroom window and they tantalized me to distraction. The following morning my breath was steaming up the store window even before it opened for business. There they were; two Stella acoustic guitars. One cost $17.00 and the one with the extra coat of lacquer cost $24.95. I begged, whined, and pleaded, and my mom finally gave in and bought me the $17.00 special.

When I got the guitar home and opened the case, I could not believe it. I had a guitar. I gently took it out of the case and ran my fingers along the wood. I just wanted to caress and stroke it. I loved the feel of it and the smell of it. I adjusted the strap and eased it reverently over my shoulders until I could feel the weight of the guitar across my back. I strode majestically to my usual spot before the mirror and saw myself for the first time. I was alone in the universe. Yet at the same time I felt like a soldier in some new army and the guitar was my rifle.

Of course, it might have helped if I knew how to play the damn thing, but at that moment who cared about such minor details? All that mattered was that I had a guitar just like Elvis. I promised my mother that I would take lessons and learn how to "really play," but after two or three sessions with my music teacher, I realized this was not working. He wanted me to learn scales. Gene Vincent didn't play scales. Chuck Berry didn't play scales. And Elvis sure as hell didn't play scales. Scales were things on fish. I wanted to rock.

In 1956, a greasy-haired kid playing a guitar was the ultimate expression of rebellion. But a greasy-haired kid playing an acoustic guitar was the worst. It was downright criminal behavior. An electric guitar was thought of as a more tasteful, stylized instrument. It was the sound of Les Paul and Chet Atkins, smooth, jazzy, and sophisticated. An acoustic guitar was backwoods and uncouth, the instrument of hicks, hillbillies, and other lost souls. It was the musical equivalent of a Chevy pickup with a bad muffler.

Since I refused to take proper lessons, I figured the easiest way to accompany my singing, which was really all I wanted to do, was to tune the guitar to an open E chord. This was so I could change chords by sliding one finger up and down the fret board, which was fine as long as I was playing major chords. Minors, sevenths, diminished, and other exotic chords that needed more than one finger to make were a challenge. But part of the fun was figuring out how to play the guitar my way instead of the correct way. Unfortunately, open E tuning condemns you to a life as a rhythm guitarist since lead parts become incredibly difficult to figure out and learning from other guitar players virtually impossible. What is ironic is that I still play that way today. I never did learn those damn scales.

By 1957, Mom and Dad were much more relaxed running the hotel. Mom became the perfect hostess, while Dad's pet project was running the bar. He had frequented a lot of bars in his day and knew what made a good one work. In a fit of inspiration he announced, "What this place needs is a new drink." Thus was born the Sputnik Fizz, an ungodly concoction of vodka, vermouth, and cherry soda with plastic swizzle sticks that had what looked like little satellites on top. It was a small but typically American attempt to cash in on the ominous Russian space program launched that year. Nobody liked the taste of the Fizz but it sold by the hundreds because of the novelty. Dad actually went Hollywood that year and took to wearing sunglasses while driving through town in his red-and-white, supercharged "Stude." I was very proud.

A few weeks later, Dad decided that the next step had to be live music. He went out and hired a local combo. They were a model Midwest polka-playing trio with a drummer and an accordionist, but the star of the show, for me anyway, was the electric guitar player who, ironically, happened to be the dreaded town barber where I had to go periodically to get "depomped." I would sneak into the bar whenever I could to watch him. He played a black-and-white Gibson and had an amazing assortment of licks and chords, which I had heard only on records and had never seen up close before. I was mesmerized. It was hard to believe that this hip guitar player was the same guy who took such sadistic pleasure in chopping off my hair.

I actually ran to get my next haircut just so I could talk to him. I could not believe it when he told me he had a spare guitar and amp that he was willing to sell me for a hundred bucks and, unbelievably, my folks went for it. God bless my folks. They should have sent me to my room, but instead they inexplicably encouraged me in my wild obsession. They put up the money so I could get a rare Slingerland electric guitar. It was an old blond, hollow-bodied, single pickup jazz guitar with a Sears and Roebuck amp. I may have been only ten years old, but I was plugged in.

Now that I had an electric guitar, I could really start copying the licks I had heard from Gene Vincent, Buddy Holly, and the Everly Brothers. Because of my age and the fact that no other kid I knew was as nuts as I was about rock and roll, I felt very isolated. But looking back on it now, the musical education I was getting during that solitude was indispensable. I am still doing things today that I learned during that time. God does work in mysterious ways.

American Bandstand also made its debut that year and put rock and roll in everybody's face five days a week. Rock and roll was everywhere and seeing rock artists became an everyday occurrence, not just on a rare *Ed Sullivan* appearance. Chuck Berry, Jerry Lee Lewis, Dion and the Belmonts, and Frankie Avalon made it look so easy. I watched *The Adventures of Ozzie and Harriet* just to see Ricky Nelson sing and play at the end of the show. And what I wanted, more than anything else, was to be one of those rock and roll guys. But all those people and places seemed so far away. There was, however, one ray of hope. A weekly televised amateur contest called *Talent Roundup* was broadcast live from WREX in Rockford, Illinois, which was only about an hour's drive from Monroe.

Every weekend auditions were held in different towns within the broadcast area, and Monroe was on the list. Miraculously, in January of 1958 these auditions were going to be held in the dining room of the Eugene Hotel. Only an act of God could have kept me away. There were lots of contestants and the try-outs lasted all weekend. Somewhere between the tap dancing yodeler and the trained parrot, I played and sang "Sugartime" by the Maguire Sisters. Even more amazing, I was chosen as one of the finalists, which meant I would actually get to perform on television. We chosen few would meet a couple of weeks later on Sunday afternoon for the exciting on-air showdown.

When the big day arrived, my folks and I showed up with high hopes at the WREX studios. I had decided to shelve "Sugartime" since I had a well-rehearsed version of "Oh Julie" by the Crescendos that I wanted to perform instead. They would be rocking in Rockford tonight.

We spent the afternoon rehearsing and getting the sound just right for the broadcast and then suddenly I was on. "Ladies and gentlemen . . . Tommy Jackson!" Things were going great until the second verse when, unbeknownst to me, something happened to the audio transmission at the TV station. I was singing just fine to the studio audience but nobody watching at home could hear a word. My mouth was moving but no sound was coming out. I found out later they even ran a ribbon on the bottom of the screen that read "Sorry . . . Technical Difficulties . . .

Please Stand By . . ." with a cartoon repairman hammering on a TV set. I guess the viewing audience that called in their votes must have heard enough, because I won the second-place prize. The girl who came in first had danced a spirited Irish jig complete with working soundtrack. At least it was not another singing guitar player.

By early spring of 1959, we had spent the better part of three years in Monroe and we were all getting weary of hotel life. The demands on my folks had become more than they had bargained for, more than they were getting paid to endure. Monroe was losing its charm and we were all ready for a change. We moved to Niles, Michigan, which was only ten miles away from our old home in South Bend. My mother's sister, Gert, lived there with her family, and we had spent so much time visiting them when I was a kid that Niles had become familiar territory. It was such a happy, normal place. Mom and Dad got their old jobs back and we found a great little two-bedroom bungalow about a block away from my aunt's house. We were all relieved to be settled in a real house.

That September I started seventh grade at Niles Junior High School. Suddenly everything felt more serious, with multiple classrooms, lockers, and upperclassmen to deal with. I even joined the choir and the school band, where I played clarinet. A few weeks into the semester I met a kid named Mike Booth, who played drums in the band. He said, "I hear you play guitar and sing. I have a full set of drums at home. What do you say we put together our own band for the variety show?"

"Hell, yes," I said. "What variety show?"

"The big one they have every year in the auditorium." Mike knew these things because he was a year ahead of me in school. I did not realize it at the time, but this chance conversation would prove to be a major turning point in my life.

I went to Mike's house after school and was thrilled to find he had everything we needed: a full set of Ludwig drums, a heated garage, and parents who pretended to be deaf. Over the next few days, we managed to enlist two more kids from our school band who played trumpet and sax, plus one of Mike's neighbors, who passed for a piano player. Even though the sound was raw and crude, playing with other musicians for the first time was a thrill. It felt powerful; it was like "being a record," especially when we were all playing in the same key.

We practiced every day after school for a solid week and learned two songs: "Lonesome Town" by Ricky Nelson and "A Thousand Stars" by Kathy Young and the Innocents. We made a try at "Angel Baby" as well but two songs were about all this outfit could handle. We called ourselves the Echoes.

The night of the variety show, we decided to go with "Lonesome Town." I remember all of us standing behind the curtain waiting to go on, so scared we could hardly talk, let alone sing. The auditorium was packed with our classmates and their parents, daring us to be good. One bad note and we could never show our faces again.

We finally heard "The Echoes" announced, and the curtain opened. There are certain moments that must be experienced firsthand to be fully appreciated, like jumping out of an airplane. This was one of them. There is a unique sound that comes from a large audience in that awkward moment between the time they first lay eyes on you and the time you actually begin to perform. It's a kind of sigh and nervous murmuring. Getting started took an eternity, or so we thought. Everything seemed to be in slow motion as we started to sing and play. "Th-th-th'ere's a place . . . where lovers go . . ." My stomach was in my throat. But once we felt the audience responding, we became more relaxed, and by the end of the song, we were actually having fun. The whole auditorium erupted into applause and some of the kids even stood up. It was intoxicating. We were a success. I do not know what would have happened if we had bombed that night, but backstage, as we congratulated each other, Mike said something I had not thought about. "We've got to keep this band together."

Mike and I met that weekend and discussed the future. We really did not know what to do next. What did staying together as a band mean? Playing for money? Making records? How do you get from Mike's garage to *American Bandstand*? The only things we had going for us were big dreams and blissful ignorance. We both instinctively knew one thing: rock and roll was guitars and drums, not horns and pianos. We needed new blood.

Mike said he knew one other good guitar player who might be interested in joining the band. He was a backyard neighbor named Larry Coverdale. Mike made a phone call and Larry came over with his Gibson Les Paul Jr. and a small Gibson amp that could shake concrete. Larry was skinny, six foot two, and eighteen years old, which was six years older than I was. Despite the difference in our ages, Larry and I had a lot in common musically. We both knew the complete works of Buddy Holly and Elvis. We could perform the entire Everly Brothers songbook from memory. It was one of those partnerships that you spend your entire life preparing for without realizing it. Within an hour, it was as if we had always been friends.

Larry may not have been the most accomplished guitar player, but he was a lot better than I was, and had already played in a couple of local rock bands. In fact, he had recently quit one because he had decided to join the navy. Fortunately for us, there was something not quite regulation about Larry's feet and he ended up flunking the physical. He was free as a bird and we netted him. From that point on we spent every available minute practicing in Mike's garage doing songs like "Image of a Girl" by Safaris and the Phantom's Band, "Hushabye" by the Mystics, and "I've Had It" by the Bellnotes.

During our rehearsals we found that since Larry could play solid leads as well as rhythm parts, we could play a lot of instrumentals like "Underwater" by the Frogmen, "Stick Shift" by the Duals, and some hard-twanging stuff by Duane Eddy. But the most amazing thing to me was that Larry could sing harmony. Up until that time, everyone in my world seemed to be tone deaf. We eventually began inventing our own two-part harmonies and began practicing songs by acts like Skip and Flip. We played "It Was I" and "Cherry Pie" and tunes like "Jennie Lee" by Jan and Arnie, who later became Jan and Dean. We did everything a three-piece band could do.

I was still playing in my open E tuning style but Larry taught me that when I stuck my finger one way it was a C chord, when I moved my finger another way it was a G chord, and so on. Larry made me musically literate and allowed me to communicate with other musicians. Of course I learned a lot of other important musical stuff, like saying "Let's take five." I learned how to count off songs—"One, two, three, four . . ."—instead of just starting and hoping for the best. We were all so excited about the band and our prospects that we hardly noticed the 1950s had ended and were gone forever.

The three of us kept on rehearsing through the first couple of months of 1960. It was such a pleasure working with Larry. What were the odds of finding another musical recluse who obviously spent as much time as I did alone in his room with a record player and a guitar learning all this stuff? We even knew the B sides to most of the hits, like "The Midnight Man," which was the flip side of "Raunchy" by Bill Justis, and "Lonesome for a Letter," which was the other side of "The Fool" by Sanford Clark. The B sides were always good to learn because most of the audiences had likely never heard them and could not tell if you were playing them right or not. Nothing went to waste.

Since we were a trio with two standard guitars, we had to compensate for our lack of a bass player. Larry would do this by playing the fat strings of his guitar while I sang and played the rhythm parts. If Larry needed to play lead, I took over the bass lines in the same way. We worked hard and eventually had enough material to fill three forty-five-minute sets.

In the life of every band there comes a moment of pragmatic self-analysis when you must honestly answer the question: "Do we stink or not?" We thought we sounded pretty good, but would anybody else think so? Were we ready for a gig? The only way to find out was to book one. Because he had worked in local bands before, Larry Coverdale knew a thing or two about Elks Clubs and Masonic Lodges. In March 1960, Larry and I went to the American Legion Hall in Niles and booked our first gig.

The Legion Hall had a grand ballroom on the main floor that was used for weddings and other large affairs. Downstairs was a bar with a dance floor that jumped pretty well on the weekends. Larry and I talked the manager into giving us a shot on Wednesday, which was a relatively quiet night. If we did well, we would get invited back. Even though it was less than a month before my thirteenth birthday, no one asked me how old I was. I guess they thought, what twelve-year-old would be seeking employment in a bar on a school night? The hard part was convincing my folks to let me do it. They were totally against it. But after a solid week of pleading, they grudgingly gave in.

A few days before the gig, the Legion Hall called Larry and told him they were going to advertise in the local papers. "What do you guys call yourself?" Larry said he would get back to them.

That night we had an impromptu band meeting. The Echoes sounded as tired as the horns and piano we had just gotten rid of. We needed a name that sounded like guitars and drums. After an agonizing three hours we decided on the Tornadoes!

On Wednesday I was a nervous wreck all day at school. That night, Larry picked me up in his beat-up, blue-and-white '53 Chevy, which immediately became the official car of the Tornadoes, since Larry was the only one of us old enough to drive. Somehow we all crammed ourselves and our equipment into the car. We decided that we would dress in white shirts, black sport coats, black slacks, black ties, and black shoes. We looked like we were going to a wake instead of a gig, but they were the only clothes we all owned that could pass for band uniforms. Even so, I thought we looked pretty sharp except for Larry, who had on white socks. There's always one in every band.

We arrived at the Legion Hall and began setting up our equipment on the postage-stamp–sized stage. In those electric, nervous moments before we went on, I felt very grown up. I wasn't scared, but it was unreal to me that I was going to be entertaining a room full of adults—for money—playing rock and roll.

At 8:00 sharp we started. We kicked off the first set with "Money" by Barrett Strong. We could tell by the look of the patrons and the bartender that they were not ready to rock and roll and that we should have opened our set with something more sedate. This became my first lesson in stagecraft. We knew right away that we had to slow it down. Our second song was the Everly Brothers' "All I Have to Do Is Dream," which seemed to bring a smile to everyone's face, and by the third song, "Poor Little Fool," people began hitting the dance floor, which made us all feel a lot better. Soon, people were coming up to the stage requesting songs, and we knew most of them. "Honky Tonk" by Bill Doggett and "Angel Baby" by Rosie and the Originals were just a couple. The one we got the most requests for was "What'd I Say" by Ray Charles.

The crowd liked us, but more important, the club manager, who was also the bartender, liked us. We each got twenty dollars for the gig. Up until then it was the most money I had ever made doing anything, and it sure beat mowing lawns. But the best thing was that they wanted us back. I had become a bona fide professional musician.

That is how it started. We played as a trio through the summer of 1960 at the Legion Hall, where we became regulars, and at teen dances around Niles, but we were getting frustrated at having to make up for a nonexistent bass player. We really needed at least one other player to round out our sound and another voice to create three-part harmonies. We found the missing element in Larry Wright, who was one of Coverdale's friends. Larry Wright played a decent guitar and he could sing. He took over as our phantom bassist using the same fat-string technique that Coverdale and I had perfected until we all finally chipped in and bought a proper bass guitar. This made a noticeable difference in our sound. We figured that if four was good, then five would be even better, and so added a sax player named Mike Finch who could belt out good solos and, just as important, owned a car. We were now two Larrys, two Mikes, two cars, and a Tom, in case you'd lost track.

The question with local bands like the Tornadoes was always the same: Can we earn enough money to make it worth everyone's while? Guys like Larry Coverdale, Mike Booth, and I were so passionate about the music that we probably would have played for no money at all. But Mike Finch and Larry Wright lived in the real world and had bills to pay. And since I was still in junior high school, we had to limit our playing to the weekends.

Even so, by 1961 the Tornadoes were playing almost every

weekend at a variety of sock hops, school dances, and the like. We were also developing a small but loyal following that seemed to show up everywhere we played. We had business cards made up: "THE TORNADOES . . . Dance Band For All Occasions!" And the phone kept ringing. We played weddings, parties, clubs, any gig we could find.

One day after school, I stopped at the Spin-It record shop in Niles, where I was a steady customer, to ask if we could put our business cards under the glass counter where other area bands advertised. The shop was owned by a very hip middle-aged woman named Edith Frucci, who everyone affectionately called Dickie. Dickie's store on Main Street was the center of the musical action in town. I also knew that she liked me and was always asking me how the band was doing. But that afternoon I walked right into the middle of an argument between Dickie and one of her clerks, who had apparently come late for work. I do not know who said what to whom but the clerk grabbed his coat and walked out the door.

The next thing I knew, Dickie walked over to me and half-jokingly said, "So, do you want a job?" Without hesitating I replied, "Yes, ma'am." And she said, "You got it." Working for Dickie at the record shop would prove to be the gateway to my career.

The job entailed a little bit of everything. I sold records and schmoozed with the customers, which was very cool. I also had to mop the floors, dust the shelves, and wash the windows, which was very uncool. I tried to time the grunge work when I figured none of my friends might stop by. Dickie always got a kick out of watching me squirm whenever I had a mop in my hand and a good-looking girl would walk in, or worse, a member of another band.

I worked after school all week and all day Saturday. But the best thing was I got to run the band out of the record shop. This was incredibly helpful. It gave the Tornadoes a lot of new contacts we would not have had otherwise. For me it was like going to Rock and Roll College. I got to know the record business from the retail side. I read all the trade papers and learned who the major players were in the record industry—the distributors, publishers, label executives, and even some of the promotion men. As a favor to Dickie, many of the other merchants in town let us put up posters in their shop windows announcing our upcoming dates. All this helped the Tornadoes compete with other area bands. And there were plenty of them.

There was a group called the Princeton Five that was terribly popular in the South Bend area. Their names might conjure up images of collegiate crooners, like the Brothers Four, but these guys were rockers. They were our nemesis. There was a group called the Playmates from La Port and the Tempests from Elkhart, and still another band from Mishawaka called the Spinners. There was even another Niles band, called the Corvettes. These were only the most popular, but this was our competition and we were the new kids on the block.

Another frustrating aspect of being in a struggling young band was the constant personnel changes. In early 1962, Mike Booth, the guy who got me into all this, got a job working weekends and had to quit. We were lucky to find a good replacement, Nelson Shepard, who had a wealth of experience playing with other bands. He had a dazzling set of red-sparkle Rogers drums and a 1960 Bonneville convertible that could blow anything off the road. Did I mention owning a car was important? We now had three of them. Plus Nelson's mother, Annette, took over our management. Mrs. Shepard was good with details, enjoyed being involved with the band, and was home all day to handle any calls.

23

In early 1962, Dickie's son Norm was going to nearby Hillsdale College and got us a gig playing a real *Animal House* frat party. It was a Friday night, two hundred bucks, and all the beer we could drink. Nobody knew I was only fourteen years old. Between the second and third set, somebody challenged me to chug-a-lug a pitcher of beer. I had never had a beer before, except the occasional sip from a relative's glass at family gatherings. I took the challenge and drank the pitcher in thirty seconds. Ten minutes later I felt like I was on another planet. The only problem was that I loved it.

The next set was incredible. My stage fright was gone. My voice sounded like thunder through the PA system and every lick on the guitar sounded brilliant, to me at least. When we played "What'd I Say" I felt like I had total command of the room. When I did the call-and-response part of the song:

> *"Hey-ay-ay!"* . . . . *"Hey-ay-ay!"*
> *"Oh-Oh!"* . . . . *"Oh-Oh!"*

The place went nuts. I felt invincible. I had found my magic elixir: Budweiser.

After the party, Coverdale was so drunk he could not drive. And since all the other guys had brought their own cars that night and I was traveling with Larry, I had to drive his rusted-out '53 Chevy all the way back to Niles. The scary part was that I had never really driven a car before, let alone navigated one down a major highway in the middle of the night, and I was nearly as high as Larry. Somehow we made it home.

In the spring of 1962, while I was working at the Spin-It, I got into a conversation with Bud Ruiter, one of Dickie's distributors. Bud worked for Singer One Stop Distribution out of Chicago. The one-stops were the capillaries of the record business and tended to be very street level in their business dealings. Bud sold records from every label to the little mom-and-pop stores on his route between Chicago and Hastings, Michigan, right out of the back of his van. As we talked, I eventually got around to the Tornadoes and told him about my band. "Well, you know," he said, "we have a recording studio over in Hastings and if we hear something good we own a little label called Northway Sound that we can release it on. I stick them in the van and put them in all my stores, on spec, of course." He handed me some samples of a country act he'd recently recorded. I did not care too much for his group but I was sure intrigued at the idea of making records.

"Would you be interested in recording my band?" I asked.

"Sure," he said. "Pick a Saturday and come over. You guys can lay some stuff down on tape and we'll see how it goes."

A couple of weeks later, we made the journey over to Hastings. As it turned out, Bud had his own mom-and-pop record shop with a recording studio in the back room. It was a nifty place with a control booth and a sound room with some decent microphones. Of course, it was mono recording all the way, but we were thrilled. We set up our instruments, Bud miked them and did a level check, and we played and sang at the same time. There was no separate tracking of the instruments and vocals.

We recorded two songs: "Judy," which was a song I wrote about the girl I was in love with at the time, and "Long Ponytail" by the Fireballs. Coverdale and I liked the Fireballs and played a lot of their tunes. We did about six takes of each song and picked the ones we liked best. We had never heard ourselves before and were pretty amazed and pleased at the way we sounded. Like wide-eyed puppies looking for a pat on the head, we asked Bud what he thought and he encouraged us by saying, "Hey, it's as good as any of the other shit out there today."

After the recording session, Bud suggested that since I was the lead singer, I incorporate my name into the band. It was something that had never come up before and I felt awkward about it, but Bud wanted it that way and no one in the band seemed to have a problem with it. So the record label read: Judy/Long Ponytail by Tom and the Tornadoes.

A few weeks later, the first hundred pressings came into the Spin-It. The labels were aqua blue with black lettering and the jacket was plain white, but to me, it was as beautiful as anything that was on Capitol or RCA. For a while I simply held on to the vinyl, bending and smelling it, feeling the seams and grooves. It had an official Northway Sound order number on it. It had all the information about the publishers and, in parentheses, under "Judy" was my name (Tom Jackson). I was actually holding a record that you could play on a record player, written and performed by me.

We put it on the in-store turntable right away and people bought it. Dickie pushed it like it was the hottest record in the country. By the end of the day, we were nearly sold out. Bud, as he agreed, put them on consignment in all the record shops he visited. We had played in some of the towns on Bud's route, which helped sales. Bud eventually pressed about three thousand copies and they did pretty well. Adopting a pattern that would often repeat itself throughout my career, we did not make much money on the deal, but we sold a lot of records.

One of the regulars that came into the Spin-It was a fellow named Frank Fabiano. Frank's dad ran the local jukebox and pinball machine concessions and Frank Jr. worked for his father. Frank Sr. was allegedly an old cohort of Al Capone who, according to rumor, set Fabiano up in business. Their operation was in Buchanan, about five miles outside Niles in a big Victorian mansion on a hill that looked like the set from *Psycho*.

Frank Jr. also managed the Corvettes, the other rock and roll band from Niles.

Frank was always hinting that he wanted to manage the Tornadoes. He always teased me that the Corvettes played better gigs than we did because he was their manager. We already had Annette Shepard as our manager and I had always kept Fabiano at arm's length, even though his remarks about our gigs were true. But now we had this record out and I was going to need Frank's help getting it on his jukeboxes, so I did not see the harm in making him something . . . say, an agent. He controlled nearly all the jukebox action within a fifty-mile radius of Niles. Now that we were "his" act, he put our record on all his jukeboxes.

Having our record on the jukeboxes was great for business and great for our ego. We even had professionally printed "title strips" with TOM AND THE TORNADOES in bright, bold letters next to the Beach Boys and the Four Seasons. And Frank did bring in some choice gigs, even if they were only Corvette rejects.

We rode "Judy" and "Long Ponytail" for as long as we could. But we had no concrete plans to make any more records. It was fun. It was a kick. But what was the point? We knew we could not break out of our little Midwest cocoon without some kind of national exposure. Why kid ourselves? We were just another local band.

In 1963, in addition to playing with the Tornadoes, I was also a fairly normal sophomore in high school looking forward, like every kid my age, to my sixteenth birthday and getting my driver's license. I was more or less going steady with a cute, petite girl named Diane who I'd met through a friend who was dating Diane's sister. I am not sure if this was a sign of the times, but she reminded me of Annette Funicello, with that short black hair and an irresistible encouraging smile that made everything seem sweet. She was everything a kid my age was looking for: tight wool sweaters, short skirts, and perfume. She was also six months older than I was, which meant she had a driver's license of her own, so she became part girlfriend and part chauffeur. Getting my own license became more than a rite of passage. I wanted to take her home at the end of the night, not have her drop me off.

In early February, I asked my folks if I could have a car since they would have to sign for it. My mother stunned me by announcing, "Your father and I have no problem with you getting a car, but we do have a problem with beer on your breath when you come home from these dances you play at. It's got to stop!" Wow, I was busted. I had no idea she knew. I sheepishly said okay and I really gave it my best . . . for a while.

My promise worked and on April 29, 1963, Dad came home with "my" car. It was a slightly rusted '57 Dodge with about 90,000 miles on it, but to me it was a Rolls-Royce. It was a big, black-and-white four-door with a gold strip down the side. It had rocket fins, whitewalls, push-button drive, and it was all mine. When you are sixteen years old, having your own car is a life-changing event. You go from teenage geek to jet-setter overnight. I drove to school every day, to the record shop after school, and to gigs on the weekends. And whenever I wasn't doing that, my friends and I were making what was called the "cruising loop" from Thomas's restaurant on US 31, back to Niles, and down Main Street to Front Street and back.

When Diane was not around, I would secretly hang out with a girl named Ginger. Even though she was a year younger than me, she was very voluptuous and tall with auburn hair. I did not feel right about what I was doing but that did not stop me.

I never meant to hurt anyone. It was just a part of being young, of being thoughtless.

That summer was the greatest. For the band and me it was the best summer yet. We played all the resort beaches up and down Lake Michigan: Silver Beach, Waco Beach, Tower Hill, and a great little combination dancehall and boathouse called Ronnie's Pavilion on Clear Lake, just outside Buchanan. It seemed like every week we had a great gig somewhere on the water.

Motown and surf music were hot that year and we did them to death. We also played "Quarter to Three" by Gary U.S. Bonds, "Wah-Watusi" by the Orlons, practically everything by the Beach Boys, "Do You Love Me" by the Contours, instrumentals like "Wipeout" by the Surfaris, "Pipeline" by the Chantays, and "Easier Said Than Done" by the Essex, but by far the most requested song that summer was "Louie Louie" by the Kingsmen, a song in which no matter how closely you listen to it, the lyrics are still unintelligible. Years later I found out even the Kingsmen did not know what the hell they were singing.

We made good money that summer. We got new outfits, powder blue dinner jackets and sharkskin suits, and new equipment. Larry Coverdale and I bought Fender guitars. I got a Jazzmaster and Larry got a Jaguar. We also bought matching piggyback amps. Larry Wright got a new Ampeg bass amp. We bought an ElectroVoice PA system with Musicaster speakers and four 664 mikes that looked like a row of chrome-plated pistols.

We had huge crowds all summer long. On a Friday night at Ronnie's Pavilion, we'd start at eight, and by midnight we usually had more than a thousand kids on a dance floor built to hold only a few hundred. Sometimes it got so packed the local fire marshals would come in and shut us down before the night was through. But that's the way it was all summer: frantic and high-voltage. In many ways, the summer of '63 was the last great summer in America. Never again would we be quite so optimistic or unapologetically carefree.

Before we knew it, summer was over and I had to start my junior year in high school. By this time Diane and I had become "pearled." I am not sure whether this tradition was confined to the Midwest, but it was beyond "pinning" a girl. You actually had to go to a jewelry store, buy a pearl pin, and give it to your sweetheart. It was about as serious as you could get in high school. It was beyond going steady. It was like being engaged to be engaged. To me the most exciting thing in the world was cheap perfume and angora sweaters. I was smitten, no doubt about it.

One day in late September, when I went to work at the Spin-It, I noticed a cardboard cutout, about eighteen inches high, on the top of the counter. The cutout had a picture of the back of four very hairy heads. It was from Capitol Records, and a caption in small print said, "The Beatles Are Coming." I remember thinking how bizarre this looked. I asked Dickie about it and she said, "One of the one-stop guys brought it in. Some new group, I guess."

I did not think much about it until a few weeks passed and that cutout was replaced by another with a picture of the same four heads, slightly turned, almost in profile so you could see ears and sideburns. The print was slightly larger and bolder but the message was the same: "The Beatles Are Coming." Kids came into the shop and started asking questions. Who were these guys? What did it all mean? We were apparently being teased. But since it was Capitol Records, I knew it must be important and that it must be going on all over the country, not just at the Spin-It. But it was still a big mystery.

* * *

On Friday, November 22, I stayed home from school in the morning with a "sore throat." Actually, it was a bit of a hangover from drinking beer the night before. By noon, I was feeling okay and decided to go to afternoon classes. I remember parking my car and walking into school during lunch break, a little before twelve. Just a normal day. I went to my locker, got my books, and walked to the cafeteria, where a friend of mine, Joe Pieta, came up to me and said, "Did you hear about Kennedy?" I said, "What do you mean?" "Kennedy's been shot."

The bell rang and I went to my next class, which was study hall. In class, nothing seemed out of the ordinary at first until my teacher, Mr. Kelly, called me over to his desk and asked me to run to the principal's office and find out how the president was doing. It usually felt great walking the halls while everyone else was in class, but this time I felt a sense of dread. When I got to the office, I saw a group of teachers and office staff huddled around a small portable radio on the receptionist's desk. And that is when I heard it. "It's official. President Kennedy is dead."

"My God," I thought. "How could this happen? Who could have done such a thing?" I was only sixteen and had never really experienced profound loss or grief. Like everybody old enough to remember, that moment was branded on my brain forever. It was a long walk back to study hall. I did not know how else to tell Mr. Kelly except to say, "He's dead." He looked at me with a sort of wild stare and said, "So help me, Jackson, if you're joking . . ." "No," I said. "It's the truth." Suddenly the loudspeaker came on. It was the assistant principal. "As some of you may already know, the president was shot today. And he is dead." A collective sigh swept over the classroom. "Classes will be suspended the rest of the day and all students may leave now." I remember just the faint shuffling of feet as everyone left the room. I do not think a word was spoken. I looked back at Mr.

Kelly. He was at his desk, slumped over with his hand on his forehead. He was shaking.

There is no need to rehash the whole macabre melodrama that transpired over the next few days. We have all seen those images a thousand times. For me, the murder of John Kennedy has remained a deep scar and a dividing line between two worlds. Twenty-seven years later, in 1990, I would spot my teacher, Mr. John Kelly, on CNN after he had become assistant secretary of state under George Bush, and our highest-ranking diplomat in the Middle East. I had my manager make contact with his office in Washington. Although we could not meet, he told my manager that he indeed remembered me from Niles High School and that horrible day in 1963.

The only thing that made December tolerable was the Beatles. The day their first single, "I Want to Hold Your Hand," was released, the heads on the cutout poster had finally turned all the way around. It was the same photo that was on the dust jacket of their new record. It was probably the best prerelease promotional campaign for a new group I have ever seen.

By January, the Beatles were everywhere. "I Want to Hold Your Hand" was number one. Several of their old singles, which had previously bombed on other labels, were now being feverishly rereleased as new recordings and were all jumping into the Top 10. Records like "She Loves You/I'll Get You" on Swan and "Please Please Me/From Me to You" on Vee-Jay. Big Top records even rereleased Del Shannon's version of "From Me to You," which he had recorded as a B side on one of his earlier hits. At one point, the Beatles actually had the top five records on the Billboard charts. Nothing like it ever happened before or since.

Coverdale and I put the Beatles under a microscope right away. In one month, we went from thinking their music was juvenile and silly to thinking they were geniuses, especially Larry, who was partial to two-part harmony groups like the Everly Brothers. He went nuts for John's and Paul's vocals. When we first started learning their songs, we were amazed at the intricacy of their chord structure and the sophistication of what, on the surface, appeared to be ditty-bop melodies. They had some magic that wore down all resistance. We learned every Beatles song that was available. We devoted an entire set to nothing but Beatles songs. We even wore Beatles wigs. As soon as the wigs went on, the girls went from dancing and chewing gum to gawking and screaming.

The Beatles opened up a floodgate and the British Invasion was on. The Dave Clark Five, the Rolling Stones, Herman's Hermits, Gerry and the Pacemakers, the Animals, the Zombies, the Kinks . . . on and on and on. And these were all big groups on big labels. We loved the new sound. It was very different from the three-chord rockers we had been playing up to that point. It was like the Russians putting up Sputnik. Up until the Beatles, we thought Americans were the masters of rock and roll.

The night the Beatles appeared on *Ed Sullivan* for the first time, the whole country was watching. It was the most hyped event in the history of television. I was at a friend's house that night and watched the show with him and his family. As they showed the individual members of the group and flashed their names and ages on the screen, under John Lennon's name ran the disclaimer "Sorry girls, he's married." My friend's dad turned to the rest of us and bellowed, "I wonder which one of those queers he's married to." That was when "the sixties" began.

This change in music was also reflected in the Tornadoes. We were so transfixed by all the new groups from Britain and so preoccupied with imitating the British rockers, that we weren't paying attention to what was going on in our own backyard.

That spring a mysterious box of records came into the Spin-It with about twenty-five copies of a song called "California Sun" by a group I had never heard of, the Rivieras. Stranger still, it was on the Riviera label, which in all likelihood meant it was a local band pressing its own records. I put it on the turntable. It sounded like a second-rate impersonation of the Princeton Five's version of "California Sun," which they had been playing for years and was practically their theme song. My antennae went up. I asked Dickie where these records had come from, and she told me a guy named Dobslaw dropped them off. "Bob Dobslaw? The manager of the Playmates?" She handed me a glossy eight-by-ten. I could not believe it. The Rivieras were really the Playmates, our old sparring partners from La Porte, Indiana. How did they do it? I grudgingly accepted the fact that another local band had had the savvy to put out a record. But I figured, what the hell difference does it make? Without national promotion or a miracle, they could not do any better than we did with "Judy" and "Long Ponytail." That all changed that Friday night when I turned on my car radio to WLS, the biggest station in the Midwest, and almost drove off the road. It was Art Roberts, WLS's top DJ, announcing as only he could, "The new smmm-mmmash hit by the Rivieras . . . Cal-La-Forn-Ya-Suuuuuun!"

I honestly did not know whether to cry or put my fist through the windshield. God, was I jealous. This could not be happening. We knew these guys. They were local schlocks, just like us. What was going on here? I had always felt that their manager, Bob Dobslaw, was a bone fide nerd who could not find his backside with both hands, but he quickly went up a few notches in my estimation. I was in a state of shock. Over the next few weeks, I helplessly watched as the record climbed relentlessly up the charts. Top 30! No, No. Top 20! Stop, Stop! Top 10! Oh my God. And not just on WLS . . . the whole damn country.

Dickie seemed to know what I was going through. She took me aside one day and we had a real heart-to-heart talk. She said, "You know, in a way, these guys have done you a big favor." "What do you mean?" "Well, if they can do it, so can you." And she was right. The Rivieras proved that with a good record and a decent distributor, even a local band could make it. That made everything a lot better but not much.

That summer, a DJ named Jack Douglas came into the Spin-It. His real name was Jack Deafenbaugh and he was the morning man at WNIL, the local radio station in Niles. He was friends with Dickie and came in regularly to buy records. We had never really talked before but on this day he specifically came to speak to me.

"Hi, I'm Jack Douglas," he said. "Do you still have your band?"

"We sure do," I said.

"You know I played your last record on my show and we got a great response to it. I know it sounds like a crackpot idea, but for a long time now I've wanted to start my own label. Would you guys be interested in recording something?"

"Hell yes," I said.

"We can record right here in Niles at the radio station. And there's a great little pressing plant in Mishawaka . . ."

It was exciting listening to him. He was serious and he had a plan. He figured he could get his regional radio friends to play anything we released as long as it was commercial and well recorded. "Who knows," he said. "With enough local airplay maybe we can break out of Chicago. At least we'll have a shot." All I kept thinking about was the Rivieras. I asked him what the name of his label was and he said, "Snap Records." And I said, "Let's do it."

As usual, many things were happening to me all at once. Mike Finch left the group to join the navy and Nelson Shepard got married and also had to quit. I kept losing guys to the realities of life. Mike and his sax were replaced by an excellent keyboard player named Craig Villeneuve and Jim Payne became our new drummer.

With the new record deal and the new band members, we thought it was time for a name change as well. We had been toying with a name that I had made up the previous year in study hall: the Shondells. We all liked the way it sounded and the way it looked when you wrote it out. And besides, back then anything with "ells" on the end of it was a potential musical brand name. The following week, when we walked into the WNIL studio for our first recording session on Snap Records, we were officially the Shondells.

We were all pleasantly surprised at how plush and modern the studio was. It was a big step up from Bud Ruiter's back room. The whole complex had thick carpeting, but we were even more amazed at all the equipment in the control booth. There were racks and racks of every electronic recording toy available at the time. Just beyond the control booth were several soundproof rooms of all different sizes where commercials were recorded and interviews taped. Douglas took us into the biggest one, which was about the size of a small bedroom, and told us to set up our equipment. He got down on his hands and knees and miked every instrument and put sound baffles between the drums and each amplifier. Jack was a good engineer. He gave us each a set of headphones with adjustable volume controls that we could plug into any of the jacks that lined the wall. God, we felt unbelievably cool. We looked at one another as if to say, "This is it!" Then came the catch.

"Oh, by the way," said Jack nonchalantly. "I know you guys want to do rock and roll, but I'd like the first single to be a little song I wrote. After that, you can do anything you want."

THUD. SILENCE. FEAR. RIGOR MORTIS.

Douglas sat down at Craig Villaneuve's electric Wurlitzer piano and proceeded to play the most godawful, inane, ridiculous, silliest piece of crap we had ever heard. It was called "Pretty Little Red Bird" and it sounded just like the title. We looked at one another in stunned silence. I cleared my throat and lied for all of us. "Ah . . . it's got possibilities."

When the realization hit us that our first release on Snap Records was going to be Mother Goose instead of rock and roll the whole mood of the session changed. But what could we do? We had heard about corruption in the recording business and of people selling their souls for the chance to make records. It was now our turn. We had to record "Pretty Little Red Bird."

We put a half-assed arrangement together and Douglas released it as our first record on Snap. The B side was a tune I had written called "Wishing Well." We spent the next six weeks praying that the record would die quickly with as little airplay as possible. We got our wish.

CHAPTER TWO

Hanky Panky

Now that summer was over and "Pretty Little Red Bird" had sunk mercifully into oblivion, I got news that hit me like a fist in the face. My girlfriend, Diane, was pregnant. Toward the end of summer 1964, Diane had been away with her parents for about three weeks somewhere in the South. We had a very emotional goodbye, and as soon as she got back she came to my house. She had never come to my house without calling before, and I was flabbergasted. When she told me that she thought she was pregnant, I was in shock. It was truly the last thing I expected. We went to a doctor and had her tested and there was no mistake. At age seventeen, I was going to be a father. It was that simple and, like it or not, things were going to change. We were both starting our senior year. We had been dating for nearly two years and we were serious about each other. We loved each other as much as two kids can, but kids is what we were and scared to death is how we felt. In the Midwest of 1964, abortion was so clandestine and unthinkable that we didn't even consider it. We were going to get married. For better or worse, I was a carouser, but when I got the news from Diane, it was like a cold shower. I tried to concentrate on school and on band business. Even though it was never a very serious romance, I stopped seeing Ginger and tried to twist myself into what I imagined was a responsible husband and father. The baby was not due until the following April, so we had a few months to prepare. Telling our parents was agonizing. We decided we would do it separately.

Telling my parents was a nightmare, but though they were upset and disappointed they also became very supportive. Whatever they could do to help, they would do it. I could count on them. Diane had a tougher time of it with her folks. They were so upset that Diane felt she didn't have any other choice but to move out. She had to stay with friends for a few weeks until I was able to work out an arrangement with Larry Coverdale and his wife. I rented a bedroom from them and Diane stayed there until we were married. We still had school to think of, but now instead of looking forward to final exams, we were trying to finalize our wedding plans. Every day I would go to school, then go to the record shop, get something to eat, and then drop by Larry's and sit with Diane as late as I could until I had to go back to my house to study. It was the kind of life you simply lived without thinking about it too much and then afterward, you wonder how the hell you did it. When I could get away for a while and be by myself, I did.

On Sunday afternoons, when I was not playing with the Shondells, I used to sneak into a local nightclub called Shula's and drink beer. After Diane's heart-stopping news, Sundays could not come fast enough. The band and I had done gigs at Shula's and the bartenders all thought I was old enough to drink. There was always a rock band on Sundays and it was usually somebody I knew. This particular September afternoon, the Spinners were playing. They were friends and I had not seen them in a while and I wanted to check them out.

One of the songs they played during their first set got an amazing reaction from the crowd. It was called "Hanky Panky."

I had never heard it before. In between sets, the drummer, Hank Randolph, came over to my table and I asked him what the story was with that song. Was it something he wrote with his brother Chuck, who was the lead guitarist? "No, we heard another band do it a few weeks ago and the crowd went nuts, so we decided to do it." They could not find a copy of the record so they were really playing whatever bits and pieces they could remember.

During the next set, over the PA system, I could hear people requesting this song over and over. The requests were coming mainly from the girls, which was always a good sign. The Spinners played "Hanky Panky" twice more that afternoon and each time the reaction was the same. The crowd went wild. Everybody hit the dance floor and sang along. I remember thinking what an unusual response this was from a normally low-key, Sunday-afternoon crowd. It was more like the reaction you would expect from a good party crowd on a Saturday night.

When I left Shula's later that afternoon, all I could think about was getting into Jack Douglas's studio and recording that song. After the Rivieras' rip-off of "California Sun" from the Princeton Five, I knew we didn't have much time and I was not going to take any chances. "Hanky Panky" was going to belong to the Shondells. As soon as I got home, I called Coverdale and Douglas and told them I had our next single.

The next day, at the Spin-It, I asked our resident musicologist, "Dr. John," who was my fellow clerk and had been with Dickie for years, if he had ever heard of a song called "Hanky Panky." "No, who's it by?" "I have no idea." The doctor got out his huge, thirty-pound retailers' guide, which listed virtually every record ever made, and looked it up. It turned out to be the flip side of a record called "That Boy John" by the Raindrops on Jubilee Records. We found out it had been released the previous fall but was almost immediately pulled off the market after the Kennedy assassination because the John in the title was JFK. (I found out later that the Raindrops were really the great Brill Building songwriting team of Jeff Barry and Ellie Greenwich.) In essence, it was the B side of a record nobody ever heard. Well, almost nobody. The Spinners had sure heard of it and so had the group who did it originally. I really felt we had to move fast.

At the rehearsal the following night, we set out to learn "Hanky Panky," except that we were as much in the dark as the Spinners as to what the words really were. All I could remember was: "My baby does the Hanky Panky." We were actually doing an imitation of the Spinners' imitation, and who knew how far the chain stretched? Since we needed more lyrics than that, Coverdale and I made up some disposable mumblings that passed for a second verse.

> *I saw her walkin' on down the line,*
> *You know I saw her for the very first time . . .*

We played it at our next couple of gigs and got the same reaction the Spinners got. Everybody loved that song. We knew we had a hold of something big. We got more requests for "Hanky Panky" than any song we had ever done, and we knew it was probably the first time any of these kids were hearing it. When we finally made it into the studio in late October, we had a tremendous sense of confidence and inevitability. We felt the song was already a hit. All we had to do was get it down on tape and the rest would take care of itself.

The session went off without a hitch. Between rewrites and the live gigs, we had made the song our own. Douglas's production was pretty clean and straightforward, with just a touch of tape reverb for echo. We did three takes and picked the second one for the A side. For the B side, we threw together an instrumental called "Thunderbolt." We listened to "Hanky Panky" over and over, and the more we heard it, the better it sounded. Douglas loved it too. "This really sounds like a smash," he said. We had finally made a record that we were proud to call our own.

Douglas made several thousand pressings, and when the first batch arrived a couple of weeks later at the Spin-It, it was a big event. Dickie pulled out all the stops and had posters and bumper stickers made up. Douglas saw to it that all the music stores in the surrounding towns had plenty of copies. He also got all his DJ buddies to give us lots of airplay. We would sit in our cars at night and scan the radio dial in hopes that some distant station would play the record, and every now and then, we actually heard it. What a great feeling it was to hear "Hanky Panky" on the way to a gig, or to and from school, or to have my friends tell me that they heard the record on such and such a station.

By Christmas, we were out of records and had to press more. It was a hit and everybody knew it. Wherever the record played, it sold. And it was Top 10 on every radio station that played it. In the Niles–South Bend area, we were number one. In most of the nearby towns, we were outselling the major artists.

Because of the local success of "Hanky Panky," we started promoting our own gigs. We went to various halls like the National Guard Armory, the Elks Club, and the American Legion Hall, and sold the managers on the idea of splitting the concessions and the take at the door. We had enough of a following by then to guarantee a good-sized crowd and everybody made money. By early 1965, we had a smartly functioning little machine going. I worked out a deal with the kids in my high school art department to make posters for our upcoming dances. We hired off-duty cops as bouncers and to work security. Several of the local papers did feature articles on us and helped promote our dates.

Yet as great as this success was, we knew that if we couldn't get the 50,000-watt stations in Chicago and Detroit to notice us, it was all going to end. In a strange way, the bigger the record got locally, the farther away we felt from the "big time." I remember thinking if we couldn't break out with a record like "Hanky Panky," what the hell could we do it with? By the end of February, it was becoming clear that "Hanky Panky" was not going to fly. All the electricity and hopefulness ground to a depressing stop.

The excitement surrounding the record had allowed me to put my situation with Diane on hold for a few weeks but reality was closing in. I began to feel like I was sleep walking, as if I were watching myself but I was somebody else. Diane and I were married on March 27, 1965. It was a small wedding at Saint Mark's Catholic Church in Niles. We were married by Father Timons, and Larry Wright was my best man. We had to take the Catholic marriage instruction course called Pre-Cana before we could get married, which was a little late in the day—Diane was eight months pregnant. My parents attended the wedding, and I think Diane's parents came as well, but if they did they stayed well in the back of the church. We moved into my folks' house, and three and a half weeks later, on April 22, exactly one week before my eighteenth birthday, I was discreetly handed a slip of paper in study hall that read: "Congratulations, it's a boy." I got permission to leave school and immediately drove to the hospital, where I saw my son, Brian Thomas Jackson, for the first time. It's very hard to appreciate certain things when you are young. As great as it was, for the first time in my life, everything I did, every decision I made, would affect other people, not just me. For the first time in my life I felt completely unqualified for this gig.

Six weeks later, I graduated, but just barely. As hard as I tried to concentrate on it, my schoolwork suffered, and if it had not been for a sympathetic teacher who gave me a merciful D minus in a must-pass civics class, I would not have made it. I remember feeling very sad that night, not only because I knew this would probably be the last time I would see most of these people, but because I was very aware that this was the end of my adolescence. For years, I had been straining to run away from my youth. I was always playing the part of being older than I was; fooling people into thinking I was not a kid. My adolescence was over and there was no going back. Just to keep things in perspective, the school hired me and the band to play at the graduation party.

After graduation, Diane, Brian, and I moved into a small one-bedroom apartment in Niles. I guess it was then, Diane resting in the bedroom, Brian colicky in his crib, a baby bottle of milk warming in a pan of hot water on the stove, that reality hit me in the face. I had to support my family. In a last-ditch attempt at normal, responsible behavior, I actually told everyone I was quitting the band, and the next day I applied for a job as a manager at a John's Bargain Store in South Bend. What was really scary was that they called me back and said I was hired. I got about halfway between Niles and South Bend and turned the car around. I could not do it. Somehow, the thought of selling curtain rods and Preparation H for the rest of my life sent a chill up my spine. Family or no family, I determined I would rather starve and be a musician.

A few days later, and still in a mist, I got an unexpected call from Hank Randolph. I thought he was finally going to scream at me for grabbing "Hanky Panky," but instead he told me that the Spinners had broken up. Hank wanted to go on the road and his brother, Chuck, did not. He asked me if I was interested in starting a new group that would travel and play six nights a week. Hank said he already had commitments from club owners

45

in the South Bend area for the whole summer. He knew several booking agents that could keep us working full-time. It would be hard, but the money would be good. And most important, no John's Bargain Store. For me, it would mean some unsettling changes because I would have to quit the record shop and the Shondells. But I was a married man with a baby. I said yes.

The only other member from the Shondells who was free to play six nights a week was Larry Coverdale. Hank said that the Spinners' old lead singer, a girl named Kathy, was also available. We were an instant quartet with Larry and me on guitars, Hank on drums, and Kathy on vocals. We called ourselves Kathy and the Koachmen. Rehearsals went smoothly. After all, each of us had been playing the same stuff for years. We sure as hell all knew "Hanky Panky."

Two weeks later, we were on stage at the High Hat Club in South Bend, a hole-in-the-wall reminiscent of the Cavern Club where the Beatles were discovered. Playing six nights a week in a club was a very different animal from playing teen dances at the YMCA on weekends. We had to be on stage promptly at the top of the hour, off stage at forty past the hour, and we were expected to play four to six sets a night. Club owners let you know real fast that you were not "playing" anymore, you were working. It was grueling work but I was making enough to feed my family and pay the rent.

Hank did a good job booking the band and we had steady work throughout the summer. In August, while playing a joint in South Bend called the Club Normandy, the owner took a shine to us and called a booking agent from Chicago to come see us. He was an old fox named Bert Wheeler and he loved us. Bert wanted to make us a real road band and he wanted us to start at the end of August at one of the clubs on the north side of Chicago called the Ups and Downs Show Lounge.

Hank and I were ecstatic. Larry was a little more subdued and Kathy gave her notice. Diane was definitely not thrilled because it meant I would be home only one night a week. But it was about a fourfold increase in pay and we figured we could do it for a few months and then take a couple of months off. We were actually just one of several dozen bands that Bert Wheeler booked throughout his Midwest club circuit. The theory was as long as you had as many clubs as you had bands, everybody stayed employed.

Because Kathy quit, we hired a sax player named Del Slade and became just the Koachmen. That summer I traded in my Dodge for a particularly ugly, olive green 1960 Chevy wagon that I thought would be good for hauling equipment. We all piled into the wagon and took off for the Ups and Downs. About three quarters of the way there, the retread peeled off the tires and the radiator exploded, but somehow we managed to limp into Chicago and found the club.

The Ups and Downs Show Lounge turned out to be a swanky supper club that catered to Mob types and high rollers. It was thoroughly intimidating to a bunch of young hick musicians. We were expected to play from eight in the evening until four in the morning in staggered sets with another act, a Latin trumpeter named Ziggy Gonzales and two go-go dancers. The dancers were dating the Mob bosses who owned the place, two bent-nosed gorillas that nobody in their right mind would argue with.

Within two weeks, Larry had had enough. He said he just could not take the insane schedule and life on the road any-more. I felt terrible. Larry was like an older brother, but for me, there was no turning back. I needed that weekly paycheck and the only place I could earn it was on the road. Hank and I had to come up with a replacement, fast. I called an old bass-playing friend named Bob King, and he came on board with another sax-playing friend of his named Jimmy Havens. Since we now had two horn players, we began doing a lot of jazz and rhythm and blues, more sophisticated material.

We played James Brown songs like "Papa's Got a Brand New Bag" and "I Got You (I Feel Good)." We made our own arrangements of Herb Alpert and the Tijuana Brass's hits like "Taste of Honey" and "Spanish Flea," plus "Watermelon Man" by Mongo Santamaria. We did a blues-jazz version of "The 'In' Crowd" as well as standard rock stuff of the day like "Hang On, Sloopy" and Bob Dylan's "Like a Rolling Stone."

For the next six months we worked constantly, six nights a week, all over the Midwest. We worked go-go clubs on Chicago's Rush Street and in towns all over Illinois, like Peoria and Waukegan. We played Muskegon and Grand Rapids, Michigan, and Davenport, Iowa. We played two to four weeks in each place. I was really worried about leaving Diane on her own with a new baby, so while I was away, Diane spent a great deal of time with my folks, who loved the idea of being grandparents. With any luck, maybe this thing would work out after all.

As if we weren't busy enough doing dates, we also began work on an album at Chicago Sound Studios. The studio was on a hot streak, having recently recorded a Top 10 single by a local group named the New Colony Six. We thought we could submit some original material to Mercury Records, which was just down the block from the studio. At least, that was the plan.

In February of 1966, we found ourselves booked in another club somewhere in Janesville, Wisconsin. One day, in the middle of our first week, the club went bankrupt. When we showed up for work that night, the doors were chained and padlocked. There was nothing to do but go home. The long drive back to Niles was awful. We felt tired and beat up. We had grown sick and tired of living out of suitcases. The only thing that made sense was to live at home and find local gigs. At least the money we were throwing away on hotels and restaurants could be invested in our album project. But it all had a hollow ring to it. I'm not sure I believed anymore.

We found a steady gig at a rather dumpy old place called the Indiana Café in South Bend. We became the house band and more or less went through the motions of enjoying ourselves four sets a night. But the truth was, we were right back where we started and we all knew it. Up until that time, whenever I hit a dead end, something unexpected always seemed to turn up. I felt as if I were walking on water, and each time I took another step the next stone suddenly appeared in front of me. This time I saw nothing.

In early April, I got an unexpected call from Dickie at the Spin-It. I had been so depressed about having to play the Indiana Café that I had not bothered to tell anyone I was home again. "Tommy, where have you been? Jack Douglas has been trying to find you. He says it's very important."

When I called Jack he was frantic. He shouted down the phone at me, "Tommy, we got a hit."

"What are you talking about?"

"Our record is number one in Pittsburgh."

"What?!"

"'Hanky Panky' is number one!"

I still did not understand what he was talking about. "Never mind," said Douglas, "just stay where you are and I'll have the people in Pittsburgh call you."

About two minutes later I got a call from a fellow who said he was a promotion man at a company called Fenway Distributors in Pittsburgh.

"Is this Tommy Jackson of the Shondells?" His voice was tense and almost out of breath.

"Yes."

"We've been looking all over for you. You're not going to believe this. . . ."

Then he told me exactly what happened. Apparently, a local dance promoter named Bob Mack, by some miracle, found the Snap recording of "Hanky Panky" in a used record bin. How our record wound up in Pittsburgh we never did figure out. Bob Mack had several dance clubs and he was always on the look-out for obscure, up-tempo rhythm and blues records to play at his clubs and keep everybody sweating, screaming, and dancing.

When he saw our record, he thought it looked like an interesting title. He listened to it, liked it, and took it along to play for the kids at his clubs. Everyone went wild, just like they had done at Shula's. The more he played it, the more everyone wanted to know about it. Who are these guys? Nobody knew. There was no history connected to it that anybody could discover. There were no other Snap recording artists.

Mack finally took his copy to Fenway Distributors, who pressed up a batch of records on their in-house Red Fox label. They circulated them throughout the Pittsburgh area and the records flew out of the stores. Mack, sensing a bonanza, called for more pressings. All the kids from his dance clubs were buying them up. By the time the local radio stations picked up on it, they could not bootleg the record fast enough. Radio switchboards all over Pittsburgh were lighting up. Within ten days, Fenway unloaded 80,000 copies and the Shondells were sitting on the charts at number one. Luckily, Douglas had put his name on the record along with place of origin—Niles, Michigan. They found him by doing what anybody would have done back in the sixties under similar circumstances. They called the center of the musical universe in a small town like Niles, the local record shop, which was the Spin-It. Dickie called Douglas and Douglas called me.

The Fenway man ended the conversation emphatically. "You've got to come out here. This is the biggest single we've ever had and Pittsburgh is a major market. This thing could break nationally."

I hung up the phone and tried to put the pieces together. I was playing covers in the Indiana Café. The Shondells did not exist anymore. I had the number one record in Pittsburgh. I was numb. I did not know what to do. I called Douglas back and he said, "Tommy, next weekend we are going to Pittsburgh—do you understand? I am picking you up at the Indiana Café next Thursday after your last set and we're leaving, so be ready."

I went to the band that night and told them the whole story. I also told them that they would have to muddle through without me over the weekend. I was going to Pittsburgh. They all wished me luck but none of them seemed particularly interested. None of them had been Shondells, and since our Bert Wheeler tour, they were through with traveling. That Thursday, Douglas showed up around midnight in his '59 Lincoln, waited until the band and I finished, and the two of us set off for Pittsburgh at around 2:00 A.M.

We drove all night on Interstate 80. It was about a seven-hour trip. I was exhausted and nervous. I tried to sleep in the backseat. The Lincoln was a nice big boat, good for sleeping, and somewhere along the way I dozed off. By nine o'clock, as we approached the city limits, I woke in the middle of a tunnel. Douglas yelled back to me, "Hey, we're in Pittsburgh."

The most amazing thing was that as soon as we came out of the tunnel, Douglas turned on the radio, and "Hanky Panky" was playing. When we tried another station, they were playing it too. We tried four stations, and the DJs were either announcing that our song was just coming up or that it had just been played. It was all over the dial. I could not believe my ears. All I remember clearly was Douglas saying over and over again, "Oh baby, oh baby."

Downtown Pittsburgh was the most confusing city I had ever been in. It was a maze of streets that all seemed to be laid out in triangles. None of them went north to south or east to west. We spent over half an hour dodging pedestrians and old-fashioned electric trolley cars until we finally found Bob Mack's office.

Mack did business in a building at the intersection of Grant and Liberty Streets and, like everything else in Pittsburgh, it was triangular; in fact, it looked like a slice of pie. It was cramped and very narrow at one end. The office was packed with people waiting to see us. The Fenway boys were there, as well as people from the local TV and radio stations, plus Mack's own crew that helped him promote all his dances. It was like walking into a beehive. Before Douglas could get a word out, Mack ran up to me and gave me a hug and said, "Tommy," like we were old friends who had not seen each other in years. Mack was skinny with a slight build but he was clearly running the show. He was very well dressed and dapper, in a sharkskin suit, with manicured nails. He was a showman all the way.

All of a sudden, everything was set in motion. Someone shuttled me over to KQV radio for the first of a series of interviews. I was pulled into a studio by a popular DJ named Chuck Brinkman, who was one of the biggest musical cheeses in town. We talked live for an hour. Then on to KDKA radio for another interview and eventually over to Channel 2 to do the Clark Race TV show. Clark Race was the Dick Clark of Pittsburgh and his show followed an *American Bandstand* format. I was interviewed again and had to lip sync "Hanky Panky." Next was the *Pittsburgh Post Gazette*, where I was interviewed yet again, this time for a feature article. Before the day was finished, I did more than a dozen interviews of one sort or another and

I hadn't even shaved in thirty-six hours. I finally got to a hotel room and collapsed.

That night, Mack, Douglas, and I had a strategy meeting and it was agreed that I would come back to Pittsburgh the following weekend for more interviews and to play at three of Mack's dance clubs. The next morning, as we were leaving Pittsburgh, "Hanky Panky" was still playing over and over on the radio. The song had set a record for most sales of any single in the city of Pittsburgh. The irony and lunacy of the last few days became clear the farther we drove from town. The record seemed to disappear. The closer we got to Niles, the more my star faded. It was like a beautiful dream receding into obscurity.

Back in Niles, Douglas and I realized that this time we would have to go to Pittsburgh with Shondells of one kind or another. The question was who? Douglas did not go for the Koachmen. He thought they were too old and too jazzy for the kind of stomping rock and roll that the creators of "Hanky Panky" would be expected to play. "You guys sound like a Vegas revue with those horns." Out of loyalty, I felt that the Koachmen should at least be given one last opportunity to turn down the offer, which they did. I cannot begin to express my depression playing for the usual bunch of weeknight drunks and how sad and frustrated I was that these guys who had been my family out on the road and from whom I learned so much were not going to be a part of "Hanky Panky."

I considered putting the original Shondells back together, but by then Jim Payne had joined the service; Larry Wright had moved away and no one could find him; Hank Randolph, from the Spinners and the Koachmen, would have been perfect except that, unlike me, married with a child, he was single and got drafted. Everyone else had either gotten married or quit the business. It would have been more trouble putting together the old band than starting with a new group of guys. And there were only a few days left before I had to return to Pittsburgh.

But Jack Douglas, who proved to have an uncanny ability for pulling rabbits out of hats, told me not to worry. Sure enough, later that week, he found a bunch of young kids who he said could pose as Shondells, at least for the coming weekend. They were a nice bunch of guys who had been playing in the South Bend area as, believe it or not, the Shandells. They reminded me of me and the Tornadoes back in the early sixties.

We put together a very lame thirty-minute set with "Hanky Panky" as the featured song, and that Saturday morning we all met at Douglas's studio and drove to Pittsburgh. I tried as best as I could to explain to Diane what was going on, but it was the same one-liner over and over: "I'm sorry, but I have to leave." By 9:00 that night we were playing the first of Mack's dance clubs, the Bethel Park Arena. We moved on to a place called the Blue Fox, and then played still another set at a club called the White Elephant. Each place held about two thousand kids and each was a madhouse. Several thousand people had to be turned away. The screaming was so deafening we could hardly hear ourselves play, which was probably a good thing. Each thirty-minute set turned into one long, extended play of "Hanky Panky" with a rock and roll standard thrown somewhere in the middle. I think we played "Money."

The first time I heard the screaming, I thought the Beatles had come in the back door. I could not get used to the fact that they were screaming for us. I had to sign autographs for the first time. I had fun debating whether I should put a twirl or an arc over the *T*. But it was truly unreal, because after years of hard work I was an overnight success, except that just beyond the city limits nobody knew my name. Mack was bright eyed and grinning. We drew the biggest crowds he had ever had. "Tommy," he said, "I'm coming to Niles next week and the two of us are flying to New York. We are going to sell 'Hanky Panky' to a major label." Jack Douglas thought that was great. Since Mack had many New York contacts, Douglas pretty much turned the operation over to him.

The following Tuesday night, Mack picked me up at the Indiana Café and we drove to O'Hare Airport in Chicago, where we caught an early-morning flight to New York. During the flight Mack said, "Tommy, you have the chance of a lifetime. If we play this right, you could be a genuine superstar." The two of us landed at Kennedy International Airport on Wednesday May 4, 1966. I had just turned nineteen.

I had never been to New York before and that is just the way I looked and felt. Until then, Manhattan had been little more than a revolving set gleaned from all the New York movies I had ever seen, which was perfect because I felt like I was in a movie. The noise was glaring and almost boastful. It was chaos in motion but always with a purpose. I thought Chicago was a big city, but you could have set Chicago down in the middle of Manhattan and it would have gotten lost in Central Park. I looked down the streets and gaped like I was at the bottom of a canyon that stretched forever in both directions. I never felt so important and insignificant at the same time.

The first thing we did was check into the City Squire Hotel at Fifty-first Street and Seventh Avenue. Mack got us two-bedroom suites with a connecting living room for meetings. We went first class all the way. I looked out my hotel window at all the taxis, thousands of them, like a yellow plague. I thought, "Who takes all these cabs?" But we had to hurry. Mack had filled the whole afternoon with appointments.

First we went to Universal Talent Agency on Fifty-seventh Street to meet a friend of Mack's named Chuck Rubin. Rubin booked most of the acts that played in Mack's clubs in Pittsburgh. He was very knowledgeable and knew the ropes in the New York music scene. Rubin told us that "Hanky Panky" was listed this week as a "Regional Breakout" in all three trade papers, *Billboard, Record World,* and *Cashbox.* The word had already hit the streets. Rubin told us it was the perfect time to go looking for a deal. The three of us then began visiting the record companies, which were all only a few blocks apart.

Columbia Records, on Fifty-second Street and Sixth Avenue, was, at the time, the biggest label, and by far the most corporate. It was like walking into an insurance company. Everyone was very polite, formal, and dressed impeccably. They all knew the story of "Hanky Panky" breaking out of Pittsburgh. They just had not heard the record. We actually had two versions now; the original Snap recording and the bootleg version, which had been sped up slightly in deference to Mack, who wanted a more frantic tempo for his dancers to "frug" to. Everyone seemed to like the fast version best. We played "Hanky Panky" for all the executives, including Ron Alexenburg of Epic Records, which was one of Columbia's big subsidiaries. Everybody wanted to do a deal. Alexenburg let us use the Columbia facilities to make tape copies so he could pass them around. I'll never forget walking into Columbia's Studio B that morning and seeing the Lovin' Spoonful in the middle of a session, working on an arrangement. It blew me away. The Spoonful were not signed with Columbia. They were only renting time at the recording studio. The Spoonful were actually signed with a new record company called Kama Sutra, and that was our next stop.

Kama Sutra was headquartered at 1650 Broadway, which was a notorious music business address. The first thing you noticed coming off the elevator was the pungent smell of marijuana. I did not know about pot firsthand yet, but it is a one-of-a-kind smell and it hit me like a brick. The receptionist whisked us right in to Artie Ripp. He was the head of Kama Sutra and he was holding court. Everybody in the room had long hair, blue jeans, beads, and headbands. And these guys were the executives. There was thick green carpeting with blue and gold stripes that went straight up the wall. There was fractured, indirect lighting shooting up behind a wraparound desk that looked like a Babylonian throne. The whole place smelled like dope. I was impressed.

"Hey," said Artie in a very laid-back drawl. "It's the 'Hanky Panky' man. Let's hear what you got." Rubin and Mack did the same song and dance they had done at Columbia. As the Kama Sutra people listened to the record, Rubin filled them in on all the details. "Record came out of nowhere. . . . Number one in Pittsburgh. . . . Biggest single sales ever . . . eighty thousand copies . . ." Our presentation was a polished and well-rehearsed act.

I say "our" presentation but it was really the Rubin and Mack show. I felt like a little kid in a room full of grown-ups. It was my record but everyone else was doing the talking. In fact, after "How do you do" I don't think I said two words. I kept being referred to as "the kid." The funny thing was that all these guys talked the same. Whether they wore Brooks Brothers suits or denims and sandals, they all had the same patter. Between being exhausted and fascinated by the whole crazy thing, I was satisfied to sit back and watch it all happen.

"Hey, man," said Artie. "That's a number one record. What kind of deal you looking for?" But Rubin, who was now thoroughly enjoying himself, stayed coy. "We're making the rounds, gentlemen, and we'll get back to you." And off we went to do it all again with George Goldner at Red Bird Records.

Meeting George Goldner was a thrill. He was a legend in the business, and I had read his name hundreds of times over the years on various 45s and in the trade papers. Goldner had started Gee, End, Rama, and Gone Records. He had discovered Frankie Lymon, Little Anthony and the Imperials, the Shangri-Las, the Dixie Cups, and a hundred other groups. And he loved "Hanky Panky" too. He also asked a lot of questions no one else bothered to ask, like "What do I have planned as a follow-up? Who owns the publishing? How much do you think it would cost to make an album?" I was slowly reaching the stage where I could not think at all. I had been up for forty-eight hours and I had to get some rest. We left Goldner and Red Bird and I went back to the City Squire and fell into a blissful sleep while Mack and Rubin continued the quest. They went to RCA, Laurie, Atlantic, and Roulette. They got a yes from every company except Roulette, whose president was out of town until that evening so they simply left a copy of the record with his secretary.

The next morning, a frantic phone call from Chuck Rubin got us out of bed in a hurry. He told us that every record company we had gone to see yesterday, the ones that had been so eager to sign us to a deal, had inexplicably called him up to tell him they were going to pass on the record. One of them, Jerry Wexler from Atlantic Records, admitted that he had received a call from Morris Levy, the president of Roulette, who informed him, "This is my fucking record! Leave it alone."

Red Schwartz, Roulette's national promotion man, had listened to the record and when Morris Levy came back, he made sure Morris listened too. They both went wild for the record. Morris was on a first-name basis with everyone in the music business and, as we later discovered, called each executive the following morning and made it clear that "Hanky Panky" would be better off at Roulette. No one disagreed. We had heard rumors about Morris Levy and Roulette—how the company was "connected" and how Morris was known as the Godfather of the music business—but the events of that morning were stunning and, frankly, a little scary. Mack and Rubin even suggested that I not attend the initial meeting at Roulette so they could straighten everything out.

About two hours later, they came back to the hotel and they were both ecstatic. All the apprehension of the morning was gone. They told me that Morris was a good man. That he needed a hit. He hadn't had a hit since the Essex's "Easier Said Than Done." "Tommy," Rubin said, "Morris wants what we all want, which is to make 'Hanky Panky' a hit nationally. And nobody knows better how to score hit singles than Morris Levy and Roulette." I was apparently being informed that Rubin and Mack had cut a deal.

Rubin said, "Listen, you've got to meet Morris in a couple of hours and sign contracts. They want to know what the name of the group is going to be. They definitely want your name out front, so . . ."

"I don't understand."

"Do you want to change your name?"

"Huh?"

"How do you want your name to read? Do you want Tommy Jackson, Jimmy Jackson, Tony Jones, John Smith, what?"

Now, I had actually been toying with the idea of changing my last name to one syllable. I wanted something easy to remember but I wanted to keep my first name and my initials. I fumbled for a second and then said the first *J* name that popped into my head. "Uh . . . Tommy . . . uh . . . James."

"So that's it then, Tommy James and the Shondells?"

"Sure."

"Great."

*   *   *

59

And that is how I got my new name. It was a twenty-second baptism. I had changed my entire personhood in the time it takes to light a cigarette. If I had second thoughts, it was too late now. Rubin was out the door.

Roulette Records was just off Broadway about two blocks from the City Squire. Mack and Rubin and I made a regal procession as we walked into the offices sharply at 3:00 P.M. There was a small reception area with a switchboard. I remember thinking it was not nearly as plush as some of the other companies we had seen the day before. Inside the main reception area, there were about a dozen small offices down a long, L-shaped hallway. The sound of phones ringing came out of every office. There was always a phone ringing in between scattered, echoing conversations, and people were constantly moving in and out of the offices. It had an immediate, visceral excitement that reminded me of being out on a New York street. As you walked down the hallway different kinds of music—Latin, rock and roll, jazz—came pouring out of every door. The walls were lined with framed gold records by pop artists like Buddy Knox, Jimmy Bowen, Joey Dee and the Starliters, Jimmie Rodgers, and jazz greats like Pearl Bailey, Joe Williams, and Count Basie. At the end of the hallway was a large suite with a separate receptionist. *Mr. Levy* was written in raised metal script on a mahogany door. This was obviously the end of the journey.

As we entered Morris's office, he was behind the desk just finishing a phone call. The voice was as New York as you could get. It was abrupt, gruff, and very guttural, from the pit of his stomach. "Okay, bubbe, talk to ya latah." We shook hands and he said, "Hey, kid, how you doin'?"—of course I was the kid again. The room was full of middle-aged men, and one by one I was introduced to them. Red Schwartz was there. The jazz great Henry Glover, who was head of A&R, was there. Murray the K, the legendary disc jockey, was there, but what was most surprising was George Goldner, who had met me the day before, said yes, and then passed on "Hanky Panky." What the hell was going on?

And there was Morris. Morris Levy looked like the pictures I had seen of Frank Fabiano Sr.'s old boss Al Capone, except that Morris was bigger and scarier. He was thirty-nine years old but he looked much older. He was very imposing and he talked and laughed in a style that commanded attention and even a kind of reverence. But there was something very likable about him. He was an average dresser, not flashy, slightly balding, six foot three, and about 230 pounds. He did not have to be at the head of the table or behind his desk for someone to know that he was the man in the room who ran the operation. I could not take my eyes off him.

After the introductions were over, I thought I would be told how all this was going to work. I expected them to tell me what the formula was for being a rock star. Instead, the conversation immediately turned absurd as Morris looked at me and said, "Okay, kid, what's next?" It took a minute for me to grasp that these music legends were actually asking me what the next move was. They were treating me like I was one of them, like I knew what I was doing. I had started thinking about what to do next only after my meeting with George Goldner the day before.

I stammered. "Well," I said, "I'm . . . ah . . . working on some new stuff for a follow-up . . . some new songs." This immediately evoked some fast praise from the chorus.

"See that, Moshe, this kid's thinking."

"How do you like that? He's already working on a follow-up."

"I told you he was a smart kid, Moshe."

Just then, in the middle of the meeting, two guys who were almost as big as Morris came into the office. They were out of breath. "Morris, we got to talk with you."

Morris excused himself and walked out into the hallway. Even though they were trying to be quiet, I could hear every word clearly. Evidently, they had just beaten up some guy in New Jersey with baseball bats who they believed was bootlegging their records. They were giving Morris the details. Everybody in the room was trying to pretend they could not hear. Red Schwartz smiled sweetly at me and began to ask deflecting questions. "So, Tommy, is this your first time in New York?"

Then the three men walked back into the office as though nothing had happened and Morris introduced me to them. One was a big guy with an Italian accent named Don and the other was an even bigger black guy named Nate McCalla, who I later learned was the president of Calla Records down the hall. "This is Tommy James. New kid. Just signed him." *Wonderful,* I thought while we all shook hands. *What am I supposed to say now? How did your beating go? Was this a business beating?* Morris must have sensed my discomfort because he walked behind me and grabbed me by the shoulders. "Relax, kid," he said with a gruff laugh that somehow smoothed into a gentle growl. He rubbed my shoulders and leaned against my ear and said, "I hope you're ready, kid, because you're about to go on one hell of a ride."

CHAPTER THREE

Say I Am

After the meeting at Roulette, we walked back to the City Squire. Bob Mack and Chuck Rubin, who had been all business up until now, suddenly relaxed. They were laughing and poking each other like schoolkids who had pulled a fast one on the teacher. The pressure was finally off. We had a deal. As we strolled down Broadway, I could not get Morris's parting words out of my head. "You're about to go on one hell of a ride." What did that mean for me? What did that mean for Diane and my son? But the day was beautiful, the sun just beginning to set, and the air was cool. Suddenly New York felt a whole lot friendlier than it had twenty-four hours ago. I was beginning to feel like this was my town.

Even though I felt on top of the world, I was still only nineteen years old. Except for this fluky record I made when I was sixteen, and the contract I had just signed without benefit of attorney or clergy, every other aspect of my new career was being handled by a bunch of middle-aged men I barely knew. I also had no idea what they were going to want from me.

When we got back to the City Squire, Mack and Rubin told me they would stay in New York for a few more days and work out the details. They told me I could go home. "Go home?" I said. "How do I do that?" "Simple," said Rubin a little impatiently. "Go downstairs, grab a cab to the Port Authority, and catch a shuttle to Newark Airport."

"Great," I said. "What's a Port Authority?"

When I finally decoded what Rubin meant, I managed to get to the airport and book a flight home. I stayed in Niles for a few days to be with Diane and Brian but my heart was in New York. And there was still this crazy problem that hadn't been resolved. Tommy James and the Shondells were a group of one. I needed to find a band, fast.

When Mack, who was acting as my manager, got back to Pittsburgh, he called me and wanted me to fly out there over the weekend to check out a group who might be "good Shondells." They were a local Pittsburgh band that played at his dance clubs. He also told me that he had stumbled across another obscure 45 in the same lucky used-record bin where he found "Hanky Panky." "It's the B side of an old single by Jimmy Gilmer and the Fireballs called 'Say I Am.' Sounds like it could be a good follow-up to 'Hanky Panky.'" Two days later, I flew out to Pittsburgh.

I met Mack's band and jammed with them a little bit. It was okay, but I did not feel any magic. That night, the guitar player took me to a little club on the outskirts of Pittsburgh called the Thunderbird Lounge. The house band was a local five-piece group called the Raconteurs, and they knocked me out. These guys looked and played great, sang like birds, and the crowd loved them. When their set was over, I was introduced to them. They knew who I was because they had seen me on the Clark Race show when I had first come to Pittsburgh. They learned "Hanky Panky" right away and it was their most requested song. We hit it off immediately.

They asked if they could introduce me from the stage and if

I would sit in with them. During their next set, they announced that Tommy James, lead singer from the Shondells, was in the audience. They brought me up on stage and we did "Hanky Panky" and a few other songs. It was like we had rehearsed them for weeks. The crowd cheered and screamed. It was a natural. I knew I wanted this band.

The next day, I told Mack that if he could get them, I wanted the Raconteurs. Mack knew who they were and said he would try to work it out. He set up a meeting in his office later that afternoon. When he got the guys together, he explained that I wanted them to be the new Shondells. Mack wanted to know if they would mind having their lives turned upside down. It would mean touring, recording, possibly fame and fortune. He needed a firm commitment. They said, yes, yes, yes, yes, and yes. Presto, I had Shondells and we were in business.

Mack called Morris and told him the news. Morris said, "Get them up here. We got to do an album right away." The next day we all went on a Shondell shopping binge to buy outfits for the band. We needed six of everything. We bought hip huggers, double-breasted sweaters and jackets, anything that was Mod, turtlenecks, dickeys, and what were then called Beatle boots, which we spray-painted gold. We were as ready for the big time as we knew how to be.

The following day, we flew from Pittsburgh to New York and headed to the City Squire, which was now becoming a base of operations and where I was on a first-name basis with everyone. After checking in, the first thing we had to do was meet at Roulette for publicity photos and shoot the album cover. The band and I made our entrance into Roulette with me in the lead and the guys following like ducklings behind. We wore gold double-breasted sweaters with white dickeys, but what turned everyone's head was our gold boots. The secretaries followed us with their mouths open, which we took to mean, "Boy, you guys are cool." We found out later that as soon as we went into Morris's office and shut the door, they all fell off their chairs laughing at us.

The first thing Morris did was introduce us to our new press agent, a tiny, assertive, husky-voiced brunette named Connie DeNave, and an emaciated, shaggy-haired photographer who looked hipper and more like a musician than we did. We all went downstairs and piled into a stretch limousine and headed for Central Park, where we took the now classic *Hanky Panky* album cover posed like pigeons in a big tree by the lake. Connie schlepped us, that was the word, all over New York, taking hundreds of publicity shots in every conceivable setting from Yankee Stadium to Greenwich Village.

After the photo shoot, we all met back at the Weinerwald restaurant across from Roulette for dinner and our first real business meeting. Henry Glover, Red Schwartz, and Bob Mack were there with Red's secretary, a very pretty girl named Ronnie, me and the Shondells, and Morris. We had the biggest table in the place. Henry had booked time at Bell Sound Studio for the following night and every night until we finished the album. I felt so excited but also content and very secure. Instead of managing every aspect of the band like I did back home, everything was being taken care of for me. All I had to concentrate on was the music, Morris would take care of everything else.

Bell Sound Studios was located on Fifty-fourth Street between Broadway and Eighth Avenue. At the time, it was an independent state-of-the-art, four-track recording studio. All the major labels used it. Years later it would be revamped as the Hit Factory. Roulette's in-house A&R man, Henry Glover, was our producer. Henry was a multitalented musician. He was a writer and arranger and had hits in the forties and fifties with jazz greats like Ella Fitzgerald and Count Basie, as well as more recent hits with Joey Dee and the Starliters. It was Henry who wrote "California Sun," the Rivieras' hit that got me so crazy back in high school.

The first night in the studio was a little chaotic. Except for the short set at the Thunderbird Lounge, the band and I had never played together. Nobody, including Henry, really knew what we were supposed to sound like, except that it should be something like the "Hanky Panky" record. Bob Mack brought his copy of "Say I Am" by Jimmy Gilmer and the Fireballs and we put it on the studio turntable. None of us had heard it before. As we listened, we all started looking at one another as if to say, "What do you think? I don't know, what do you think?"

It was a three-chord ditty reminiscent of "Hang On, Sloopy." Not bad . . . not great . . . but not bad. It had room for a lot of guitar work. It had possibilities. And it had a real teen, pop dance feel to it. Mack may have been on to something. We played it three or four times and then started playing along with the record, note for note, until we finally turned off the record and it was just us. The engineer pushed the record button. We did about six takes and picked the one we liked best and that was that. When we heard the finished playback, we actually liked our version better than that of the Fireballs.

"Hanky Panky" had been out for only three weeks but it was already in the Top 30 on the charts. It was doing what everybody had predicted it would do, explode! We needed a good follow-up, fast, and now we had it. Finding "Say I Am" was a stroke of luck.

From that point on, the making of the *Hanky Panky* album turned into a two-week party. Once we had our follow-up in the can, all the pressure was off and everybody could relax. Red Schwartz brought the entire Roulette staff down to the studio.

Ronnie and the rest of the secretaries came down with all the other executives except Morris. Everybody was clapping, singing along, or just hanging out in the control booths. We were the winning football team and they were the cheerleaders. You could tell that Roulette was hungry for a hit, and it felt good to know that we were it.

Over the next few nights, the album really began to take shape. The more the guys and I played together, the tighter the music got. I loved Joe Kessler's guitar work. He played a Fender Jaguar through a souped-up Kustom amp, a real cheap amp actually, with a built-in vibrato unit. It sounded perfect for what we were doing. It sounded like he was tickling the strings rather than picking them. Ronnie Rossman played a Hammond B-3 organ and a second keyboard called a Chordovox, which was actually an electrified accordion on a stand that had an almost toylike quality to it. George Magura had an octave splitter that made his saxophone sound like an entire brass section, and Vinnie Pietropaoli was as good a rock drummer as I ever heard. I can still see him sitting in the drum bay surrounded sideways and top with baffles. But Mike Vale, the bass player, and I really hit it off. He became sort of second in command and middleman between me and the group. If there was a problem, Mike handled it. I played rhythm guitar and sang most of the leads. Mike had a good voice and sang lead on a couple of tracks.

The album became a mix of cover songs and originals. We did a song I wrote called "Don't Throw Our Love Away," plus a couple that the band had written by themselves: "The Lover" and "Soul Searchin' Baby." As we picked the cover songs, the album took on a real R&B feel. We did "I'll Go Crazy" by James Brown, "Good Lovin'" by the Rascals, "I'm So Proud" by the Impressions, and "Cleo's Mood" by Junior Walker and the All Stars. We also did a song from Morris's publishing company called "Lots of Pretty Girls," which was destined to be the B side of "Say I Am" because, well, Morris owned it.

In spite of the rush job, the *Hanky Panky* album was not half-bad. The band and I recorded eleven songs, with the original "Hanky Panky" being the twelfth cut. The B side of the original single, Larry Coverdale's instrumental "Thunderbolt," was dropped from the album. While we all worked on the album at night, I spent most afternoons with Red Schwartz, who became my guru and mentor. He was the quintessential rock and roll promo man.

Red was in his mid-forties, tall and lean with Creamsicle-colored hair that had been red once upon a time. The life of the party, Red was extroverted and had a quick, snappy, East Coast banter as funny as any stand-up comic. Red was up on all the latest fads. He would work all day at Roulette in a business suit and then show up at some hip nightspot wearing a Nehru jacket and a gold medallion. Red wore his midlife crisis like his toupee; you hardly noticed it. Morris's secretary, Karen, told me that she was with Red once on the beach and he took off his toupee for some reason. He went from forty to eighty years old in seconds flat.

By the time I met him, Red was already a legend in the business. Before coming to Roulette, he had been the only white DJ at an R&B radio station in Philadelphia. When Vee-Jay records out of Chicago discovered Red was responsible for about 90 percent of their sales in Philly, they hired him as head of promotion. Red had hits with artists as varied as Jerry Butler and the Four Seasons. He even signed the Beatles to their first American record deal before anybody had ever heard of them. Being with Red was like taking a crash course in professional schmoozing, and he had it down to a science. During those first few weeks, Red and I talked to virtually every major radio program director in the country. At Roulette, everybody from Morris on down constantly worked the phones. Karen's job as Morris's secretary was fending off anywhere from 100 to 150 calls a day by people intent on talking to Moshe. Red's script was simple. He would get a DJ or program director on the phone and talk up "Hanky Panky." Halfway through the conversation, Red would say, "Guess who just walked into my office? Tommy James!" And then he would hand me the phone. I would turn on the charm for a few minutes and hand it back to Red. We did this all day, every day, until the album was finished.

Once the album was done, a national tour was put together by a talent agency Morris had lined up for us: Associated Booking Corporation. At the time, ABC was as big as William Morris, and Sol Safian was one of their nimblest agents. Booking one-night stands is a nightmare of logistics, and Sol was the best one-nighter booking agent in the country, and he was our man. Our first date was a local gig in Yonkers, and Red came with us. We were slated to follow a little house band. They were just kids, and I remember bragging, "Red, we're going to blow these guys right off the stage." Red looked at me and said, "Calm down, kid. Five minutes ago you *were* those guys."

Sol and ABC lined up a slew of dates starting in New England with the aim of working the entire country, one region at a time. Of course we were going to need a lot of cash for road expenses, travel, and such. Since we had yet to see anything resembling a paycheck, I was going to have to ask Morris for a serious cash advance. I called up Karen to make an appointment for the following afternoon. "Morris can see you at one o'clock. Make sure you're on time."

Since I had signed with Roulette, and considering how I had come to be here, I'd begun making inquiries about Morris to anybody who would talk to me. This is what I quickly learned. Morris was born in 1927 and grew up in the Bronx. He was a Jewish-Spanish mongrel with a touch of the poet in him—a very little touch, but a touch nonetheless. He was thrown out of fourth grade and sent to reform school for punching his teacher in the nose. He worked the rackets for the Mob while he was a teenager, and never lost their phone numbers. After a stint in the navy, he became a "darkroom boy," working the photo concessions in a string of Mob-owned nightclubs all over New York and New Jersey until he was finally able to buy his own club, Birdland, which he transformed into the most famous jazz club in history. He started his own publishing company by getting George Shearing to write and give him publishing rights to a theme song for the club, "Lullaby of Birdland," one of the most famous jazz songs in history. His publishing business soon became an empire. All this, before he reached the age of thirty.

In 1956, Morris formed an alliance with the record producer George Goldner to take advantage of the new and exploding rock and roll market and exploit Morris's huge song catalog. Together, they became involved in a batch of new record labels, including Roulette, Gee, Gone, End, and Rama, and signed a phenomenally successful stable of acts that kept them in hit records for years. They included Jimmy Bowen, Buddy Knox, Jimmie Rodgers, Frankie Lymon and the Teenagers, Little Anthony and the Imperials, the Flamingos, and the Chantels. He also created Tico Records to service the Latin market and later Calla Records for the R&B crowd, run by his friend, bodyguard, and enforcer Nate McCalla. Morris was one of the first entrepreneurs to market and sell rock and roll to teenagers. He seemed to have a knack for understanding hit singles and the new environment of Top 40 radio, which began in the mid-fifties.

Morris was also instrumental in bringing Alan Freed from Cleveland to New York, where he set Freed up at WINS radio. In a matter of months, Freed was the number one disc jockey in New York, and therefore in America. By bankrolling Goldner and Freed, Morris became the center of the music scene. At one point, Morris and Alan actually tried to copyright the term *rock and roll,* and they almost pulled it off. The saying was: George made them; Alan played them; Morris paid them . . . sometimes. That was the way the machine worked.

When the payola scandals hit in the late fifties, Morris and Alan were right in the thick of it. The spotlight was on two main targets: Dick Clark and Alan Freed. Dick Clark actually did have some investments in the music business, which he promptly sold, presenting himself as a clean straight guy, and got off the hook. Alan Freed was just the opposite. He was loud and pugnacious, and when Congress found out that Morris was not only the money behind the music, but also held the deeds to Freed's homes, Alan took the fall. Already in bad health from a drinking problem, he died broke and broken, near penniless a few years later. Morris, on the other hand, thrived.

By the end of the 1950s, George Goldner's horseracing fetish left him nearly broke. In order to keep his head above water, he sold his interests in everything to Morris for, shall we say, a song. Morris, who had a genius for exploiting the weaknesses in other people, was only too happy to oblige, and he became the sole owner of this musical empire.

Morris continued to sell millions of records in the sixties with acts like Joey Dee and the Starliters, the Cleftones, Lou Christie, the Essex, and the Hullabaloos. These were the records I sold every day at the Spin-It back in Niles. The 45 r.p.m. single was the fuel that drove the record business, and one thing Morris and Roulette did better than anyone else was sell singles. Chuck

Rubin was right about that. Singles were Roulette's bread and butter. Albums were an afterthought. There was no such thing as a concept album with Morris unless it was the cutout albums, the record industry's version of the used-car business, which made him rich and was a concept that he invented. Otherwise, albums were what you sold after you sold the single. Morris Levy sold music by the pound.

All this was information that I found out through Red, Henry, Chuck Rubin, and Ronnie and some of the other secretaries. I still could not figure out who the other quiet, serious men were who visited Morris on a daily basis. The men who did not have an office. I tried to press Karen for information. Karen was every nineteen-year-old boy's dream. She was a beautiful blond who ran the place with authority and charm. She answered to no one except Morris, and Morris kept her moving. His baritone would boom out into the waiting room, "Karen, get me coffee. Karen, get me Artie Ripp on the phone." You could always tell what kind of mood Morris was in by his last phone call. When he was pleased or accessible it was "Okay, bubbe, you got it." When he was angry it was "What the fuck are you guys trying to pull over there?" Lots of obscenities, but the real obscenity was in the style and tone more than in the words. Morris did not need four-letter words to scare you. Sometimes "C'mere" was enough. The place resounded with his voice and presence. The floor could rattle. And Morris was never at his best when he knew you wanted to talk money. As often happened, Tommy Eboli or Tommy Ryan was in with Morris.

"What's his name," I asked Karen. "Eboli or Ryan?"

"Both."

"Yeah, but who is he?"

Karen, in a low voice, started to tell me a capsule version of Tommy's career. It was like listening to reruns of the *Untouch-*

ables. "Way back in the twenties there was a guy named Joe 'the Boss' Masseria, He was shot by Salvatore Maranzano. Then, I think Lucky Luciano shot Salvatore and had to go to prison, so Vito Genovese took over. Well, when he went to prison, Frank Costello took over, but Vito didn't like that so they got Vinnie Gigante to bump off Frank but they just grazed him."

"But if Vito was in jail, who arranged to have Frank Costello killed?" She just pointed her thumb at Morris's door. "That's why Tommy's kind of running things now." Not for the first time did I wonder, *Oh my God, what have I gotten myself into?*

About one o'clock, Morris's door opened and Tommy Eboli walked out. Quiet and serious as usual, he gave me a polite, almost friendly nod. "You can go in to see Morris now." As I started walking in, I saw Eboli go behind Karen and gently rub her shoulders.

As I walked into the inner sanctum, I glanced at some of Morris's favorite memorabilia on the walls. His portrait with his arm around Cardinal Spellman. The sign that read, "O Lord, Give Me a Bastard with Talent." The various plaques he had received for humanitarian work he did for the United Jewish Appeal and other charities. It was more like having an audience than a meeting.

"C'mere, kid. Sit down. What do you need?" This was the first time I'd had to deal with Morris one on one. It was the beginning of an ongoing head game between us as to how much I was costing him versus how much I was making for him.

"Well," I said. "We're going on the road and we need some cash for expenses."

"What?" Morris would start to get very rough, quickly. "Hotel bills, studio bills, you know how much you guys already cost me? Now you want more?" All through this chiding I could only sit and reflect. We had just released a hit single that was pretty certain to climb to number one. We had completed an album in less than two weeks that was almost guaranteed to go gold. And since I learned very quickly that most of the expenses were going to come out of my pocket against royalties, it was probably one of the cheapest albums ever made. And now, at his command, we were going out on a promotional tour to sell his records.

"What are you doing to me, kid?" The voice was relentless, booming on and on, rough and threatening. I held firm. It was sort of white-knuckle firm, like when you grip the armrest because you know the plane is going down. This was how you did business with Morris.

All of a sudden the haranguing stopped. I had been delivered the lecture for the day and now we got back to business. "Karen," the voice erupting out of the office door, "cut Tommy a check for ten grand." That was the way it would always happen. First he would pulverize you, than he would end up giving you the money. Later on, I would get better at these encounters, but this first one left me drained.

As I left the office Morris said, "Hey, kid, don't be a stranger. Call every once in a while." Ever the concerned parent. On the way out of the building, I stopped by Red's office, and he handed me a box of "Hanky Panky" singles to take with me on the road. I was so busy cutting the album and working the phones that I had not had a chance to see a commercial copy of the record on Roulette until now. It was good news and bad news. The good news was that my name was on a monster hit on a major label. The bad news was that Bob Mack, without saying a word to me, had gotten Morris to print "Bob Mack Presents" above the title, implying that it was all Mack's show. I was furious. I also found out from Red that Mack had received a lot of money from Morris for the sale of the master. No one could yet account for any money from the sale of the 80,000 bootleg copies that had sold so well in Pittsburgh. And I had just had to beg for road money. I tried to keep my cool but it was tough. The next day, the Shondells and I rented a station wagon and a U-Haul trailer to lug the equipment and headed north toward New England.

There were no seasoned road warriors on this trip. The only road experience I had ever known was when I traveled the Midwest with Bob King during those months back in 1965 after I graduated high school. The new Shondells had even less experience, but they were not prima donnas. They got right in the trenches with me. They knew how to take care of business and each guy had his own area of expertise. Ronnie Rossman had a knack for details, like arranging hotel reservations and collecting the money for the gigs. Mike ran the scheduling and rehearsals and kept the other band members in line. Somebody else was good with maps and directions; God knows I wasn't. I was in charge of the wallet, which allowed for special status and longer nap time. They were good guys and they understood the pressure I was under.

When you are promoting your first record, the first dates are always the worst. Even though "Hanky Panky" was a huge radio hit, we were still an unknown band. Our opening dates were a string of open-air nightclubs called the Surf Ballrooms. These clubs had been built during the big-band era and ran up and down the New England coastline. They each held about five thousand people. Even though they were considered the low end of the food chain for any group with a hit, they turned out to be fun dates.

For the next three weeks, we worked from Connecticut up to Maine, playing the Surfs and other rock clubs. They were all one-nighters. Just what ABC was famous for. We worked five to six nights a week and usually did two shows a night. During the long drives between dates, we had the radio on nonstop. Top 40 AM all the way. While listening for "Hanky Panky" we got to know every lick of every other song that summer: "Cherry Cherry," "Wild Thing," "Little Red Riding Hood," "Summer in the City," "Red Rubber Ball," "Sweet Pea," "Black Is Black," "Along Comes Mary," "96 Tears," and on and on.

Every time "Hanky Panky" came on the radio, I had to laugh. How in the world did this silly little record ever get on the radio with all these monster hits? It was unreal, and yet here I was on the road with five guys I barely knew masquerading as the group who made the record. I thought often of Larry Coverdale, Jack Douglas, Dickie and the record shop, my wife, Diane, and my son, Brian, and all the other people who really made this happen. Not one of them was with me.

Any ideas I had about the glamour of rock and roll went right out the window like a cigarette butt. Traveling the country, in the summer, with five sweaty guys and no air-conditioning is no picnic. The car developed a permanent odor of greasy French fries, old socks, and bits and pieces of aromatic oddities undefined but acquired along the way. The ashtrays overflowed with cigarettes and the plastic seats were hemorrhoid factories. There were stains whose origins you did not want to know about. By the end of the first week, that station wagon had become a slum on wheels.

Normally, we would pull into town by early afternoon. The first thing I would do, once I got to my hotel room, was call Red Schwartz. Red would give me daily updates on "Hanky Panky" and a list of interviews I would have to do that afternoon with the local radio stations and newspapers. Usually I would phone them in but sometimes the newspaper people would be waiting for us at the hotel. While I would be schmoozing with the press, the guys would be down at the venue setting up for the night's show. In the summer of 1966, roadies had not been invented yet.

By the second week, we had developed a pretty good system. None of us had ever worked this hard before. We were sore all over and our voices were shot to hell. We were all beginning to sound like little Morris Levys. The following day we would load up the U-Haul and drive to the next town and start the whole procedure all over again. Red told us everywhere we played there was a major spike in sales. The tour was beginning to look like a success, and as a result, new and better dates were pouring in. If I had to work such a schedule today, in one week they would take me away in a body bag. When you are nineteen years old and promoting your first national hit record, it is easy to convince yourself you're having fun.

The Northeast leg of our tour ended just after the Fourth of July weekend in Troy, New York. We were scheduled to fly to Alabama the next day to play two big shows for WBAM radio in Birmingham and its sister station in Montgomery. These were our first big arena dates, the Big Bam shows as they were called, and we were on the bill with Herman's Hermits and the Animals in both cities. Not only were these bands heroes of mine, but the radio stations sponsoring the shows were key stations in the South.

The day before we were supposed to leave, there was a national airline strike and all air travel was suspended. Red was frantic. "You've got to get there. I don't care if you have to crawl." So after we finished the show in Troy, we did the only thing we could. We packed the U-Haul, drank a lot of coffee, piled into the station wagon, and headed for Alabama. All I remember is trying to sleep in the backseat with my mouth and the windows wide open. Each time we got pulled over by the cops for speeding, I would wake up with bugs and gravel in my throat. Somehow we made it. We got to Montgomery about two hours before show time, no sleep, no hotel, no shower, and went right to the arena.

The first person I ran into was Eric Burdon of the Animals standing, almost posing, by himself in a dressing room doorway. I went up and introduced myself, even stuck out my hand. He looked at me as if to say, "Who the bloody hell are you?" He was like a pit bull that snarled every time you tried to pet it. Of course, what did I expect? The guy was an animal.

Peter Noone, on the other hand, could not have been nicer. I was a little shy about introducing myself after Eric's growling but Peter was terrific. He went on and on about how much he loved "Hanky Panky." The Hermits were great guys too. We made plans to meet after the show. Sleep or no sleep, we were going to party with Herman's Hermits.

As the arena began to fill up, you could hear the noise of the crowd from backstage. It was electric. We were the opening act and it was the biggest crowd we had ever played before, nearly 30,000 people. The stage was an immense rectangle glutted with scaffolding and hundreds of klieg lights and a sound system on a board that looked like the skyline of New York at night. Because it was so big, we ran on stage as soon as we were introduced, grabbed our instruments, and started playing before the applause died down. The eruption from the crowd was louder than expected but the lights were so blinding, we could not see the audience, we only heard them.

"Hanky Panky" was now in the Top 10 and was a big enough hit to brand us legitimate stars in the eyes of any audience. We got more screams than we'd ever had before. Screaming, by the way, was how groups compared themselves to one another. The more screams you got, the bigger you were. At least that's what we told ourselves.

After our set was over, I became a fan again and caught every song the Animals and the Hermits did. It was incredible to be backstage listening to all those hits back to back. I felt like an amateur next to these guys; me, with my little up-and-coming hit, next to all that gold. As I listened, I couldn't help thinking I sold every one of their records at the Spin-It in Niles and now I was working with them. After the show, we got together at the local Holiday Inn pool bar, where we were all staying. It was me and the Shondells and the Hermits having a great time on one side of the pool, and the Animals, belligerent and surly, on the other side. You had to love them, though; they were the same offstage as on.

The next night in Birmingham was an even bigger bash than Montgomery. Limousines picked us up at the hotel, so for once we did not have to take the station wagon. There was a huge press conference before the show; lots of snapshots and interviews between the hors d'oeuvres. We were really getting spoiled. It would be tough going back to ballrooms and small clubs after this. Those two days in Alabama left a lasting impression on us because it was how we measured the rest of our gigs. After a few more dates in the South, we ended up in Atlanta. The airlines were still on strike and the green station wagon was becoming rancid, but we soldiered on and did another marathon drive to our next stop on the tour, a huge gig in Chicago.

We were now into the third week of July 1966, and "Hanky Panky" finally hit number one on the charts. For most of that month, a battle was raging between "Strangers in the Night" by Frank Sinatra and "Paperback Writer" by the Beatles, but "Hanky Panky" came along and trumped them both. We drove up the interstate listening nonstop to the two big Chicago stations, WLS and WCFL. WLS was our beacon. Not only were they playing "Hanky Panky" to death, they were also relentlessly plugging our upcoming date at McCormick Place in Chicago. Red was obviously back at Roulette working the phones nonstop.

But even more exciting was hearing our new record, "Say I Am," on the radio for the first time. Roulette had just released it and Red had given WLS a "world exclusive." I remember thinking what a brilliant move it was giving WLS a vested interest in breaking our new record the very week we were going to be in Chicago. I loved "Hanky Panky," but to be honest, I had been living with that song for more than three years. It was so good to hear something else on the radio. And this time, the guys had a stake in it because they were actually on the record. We drove all night and heard "Say I Am" at least once an hour. They were referring to it as the new smash by Tommy James and the Shondells.

When we finally saw the Chicago skyline come into view, it hit me just how unbelievable all this was. If anybody had told me eight months ago, while I was beating my brains out playing go-go clubs on Rush Street, that by the following summer I would have the number one record in the country and would be staying at the swankiest hotel overlooking Lake Michigan, and headlining the biggest rock show of the year, I would have told them they were crazy.

With the Beatles coming into town the following week on what was to be their final tour, the energy in Chicago was electric. The release of "Say I Am" came at the perfect time because the McCormick Place gig was a little intimidating for us. The event was called the World Teen Fair and we were going to be bumping heads with some of the biggest acts in the business, most of whom had more hits than we did. Bands from all over the world were on the bill or playing the Chicago area during the next couple of weeks. The Mamas and the Papas, Simon and Garfunkel, the Lovin' Spoonful, the Association, the Dave Clark Five, the Shadows of Knight, Martha and the Vandellas, Chad and Jeremy, our old friends the Animals and Herman's Hermits, the Standells (who were actually from Boston but goofed on everybody by speaking with fake British accents), the Outsiders, the New Colony Six, Sonny and Cher, even Stan Musial was going to be there signing autographs. We would be playing at different times and on different stages, but this time, Tommy James and the Shondells were getting top billing.

We pulled up to the Executive Hotel on Michigan Avenue. There were screaming girls out front rushing up to us with things to sign. There were more screaming girls in the lobby. There were photographers from the newspapers, and at the desk there was a mountain of messages, mostly from Red Schwartz, that had to be answered. Before I went up to my room, I called Red from the lobby pay phone. He was more excited than I was. Roulette had gotten an initial order from All State Distributors in Chicago for 50,000 copies of "Say I Am," which was an unheard of number of records for a song that had only been on the air for forty-eight hours. We had two chart hits at once in Chicago.

Red had a laundry list of DJs, promo guys, and distributors I would have to talk with. As he rattled off an alphabet soup of station call letters, I was frantically trying to write everything down on a hotel napkin. Red had promised the stations that I would do live interviews with them in exchange for them playing "Say I Am" the following week. Red said, "Listen, man, we can bust this record wide open by next week but you have to make these calls. Don't make me look like a schmuck."

McCormick Place, the site of this weeklong rock festival, was a gigantic complex of arenas and exhibition halls. The show's sponsors expected up to half a million people but during the four days that we headlined it was closer to a million. Opening night was fantastic. There were more than 25,000 people pressed against the stage, rocking back and forth. We were no longer the one-hit-wonder kids. The release of our second record seemed to give us real star status. We got screams that night like we'd never heard before.

When the show was over, we were surrounded by the Chicago police, all grimly determined to see us safely to our dressing rooms amid thousands of screaming teenage girls. Waiting for us in the dressing rooms was another horde of reporters and photographers. Everybody was shoving microphones in our faces, asking everything from our opinions on social issues and the meaning of life to what kind of chicks turned us on.

This heady adulation went on for the next three days, and I must say that it is awfully easy to get cocky when everybody around you is telling you how great you are. But the funny thing about this band was that every time we got to thinking we were too cool, something would always happen to bring us back down to earth. Our last night in Chicago would go down in Shondells history as the "Oh My God" show.

Our set began as usual. We hit the stage in our green, iridescent Mod sharkskin suits and favorite gold Beatle boots. Our act was basically all the songs from our first album. We kicked off with "I'll Go Crazy" then went into hyperdrive with "Shake a Tail Feather" followed by "Say I Am," then we would mix things up a bit. George would put down his sax and play Mike's bass. I would grab a tambourine and hand Mike the lead microphone and he would sing the two songs he sang on the album, "I'm So Proud" and "Love Makes the World Go Round." What I did not know was that he had been practicing some slick new moves and had not bothered to tell anyone.

In the middle of the second song, Mike dramatically slid on his knees to the front of the stage and grabbed the outstretched hand of one of the shrieking teenyboppers in the first row, at which point the crotch of his pants split from his rear end to his belt buckle. At that moment we all learned something else about Mike we had not known. He didn't wear underwear. Not only us but now most of the people in the first ten rows knew it too. He gave "hanging out with the band" a whole new meaning. Whatever shortcomings Mike may have had as a singer, he more than made up for that night with, shall we say, showmanship.

As the girls were being whisked away by their protective mothers, Mike dived behind his bass amp like Pete Rose flying headfirst into third base. And that was where he stayed for the rest of the gig.

CHAPTER FOUR

I Think We're Alone Now

By the end of August, our summer '66 tour was over. The Shondells went home to Pittsburgh and I flew back to New York. My first stop was Roulette. It was like walking into a beehive. On my way to see Morris, I heard my name coming out of every office:

"We're working on the next Tommy James single now."

"I want a full-page ad on Tommy James by next week."

"No, Tommy's not available until the middle of September."

I was getting the impression that Tommy James and the Shondells were not just Roulette's new project, we were their only project. The funny thing was that through all this commotion, everyone seemed oblivious to the fact that I was standing there. Finally Red Schwartz called me into his office. "Listen," he said, "we have to do the trade and the teen magazines this week and you have to get with Henry Glover about the next single." Before I could answer, Henry walked in and grabbed me and pulled me into his office. "Morris wants to get the next single ready." Henry pointed to a three-foot-high stack of acetates.

"Listen to these and see if there is anything you like. If not, we'll get you another stack." Henry was never out of stacks.

Next I passed Normand Kurtz's office. Normand was Morris's in-house lawyer for music deals. Normand told me he was putting together a foreign distribution deal to release my whole catalog overseas. My whole catalog? I didn't even know I had a catalog. Normand had cut his teeth in the record business working for Linda Eastman's father, Lee, whose real name was Leopold Epstein. It's hard to figure which profession has the most characters with aliases, show business or the Mob. Normand was a perfect Roulette employee. He was as big, gruff, and street smart as any of the boys who hung out in Morris's office.

I walked by Gerry Cousins's office and thought I might as well try her too. Gerry was the sales manager and struck me as far too normal and well adjusted to be working at Roulette. She was on the phone and muffled it for a second. "Tommy, we just did eight hundred thousand with 'Say I Am.' Isn't that great?" I gave a thumbs-up as I walked out and marched inexorably toward the end of the hall. Just before Morris's office was a little cubbyhole containing Howard Fisher, the comptroller. Unlike everybody else in this place, Howard always looked like a beaten hound dog, always weary, disheveled, and overburdened. His job was to collect and disperse Morris's money. No wonder he looked so miserable. And then there was Morris.

When I walked into the reception room, I could hear Morris on the phone, growling and swearing as usual. Karen gave me a wink and waved me in, and I gingerly took a seat. Morris slammed the phone down and said, "Making you a fucking star is going to kill me." He leaned back in his chair. "Well, we're doing good," he said. "Just don't get the idea the second record is going to be as big as the first." Vintage Morris. No pleasantries. No slap on the back. No mention of the tour we'd just busted our ass doing. "We need the next record," he said.

I began realizing that coming up with the next record was always going to be the essence of my relationship with this guy. It was like having to throw red meat to a hungry tiger at regular intervals in the hope that he won't eat you. There never seemed to be any time to just enjoy the current success. There wasn't any rest at all until the next single was in the can. "We're working on a couple of new things," I said, "and Henry just gave me a bunch of stuff to listen to." Of course, I had absolutely no faith in Henry's stack of dusty demos. "Well, make it fast," said Morris. "We need another album too."

Another album? The *Hanky Panky* LP had been out only a month and he wanted another one? My mood swung from cool confidence to panic. It was the first time I was really beginning to feel that I was in over my head. I just did not want Morris to know it. "No problem," I said. "I'll get the guys up and we'll start right away."

I walked out of Morris's office in a daze. That was the moment I realized that when you boil it all down, I was doing this thing on my own. Oh, I could always get fatherly advice from Red and production tips from Henry, but what was painfully clear was that if I didn't come up with the magic, nobody else was going to. As I passed Fisher's office on the way out, he suddenly looked normal to me.

A couple of days later, the band and I met in Glover's office to plan the next album. Much to our displeasure, in addition to the acetates I already did not like, Henry had a new pile of crap that Morris was insistent we do. They were oldies from his catalog like "Ya Ya," "Fannie Mae," and "Shout." An album full of this stuff could easily have me back in Niles playing the Elks Club within six months. We all felt that if we were just given a few weeks we could write enough songs ourselves to put a decent album together. But no one at Roulette was willing to challenge Morris. So off we marched to Bell Sound Studios to start recording.

It was like grinding out hamburger meat. The first album had been so much fun. We were allowed to be ourselves while Henry was basically a creative spectator. But with the added pressure from Morris, Henry was now very uptight and intent on doing things his way. Unfortunately, that meant a lot of very stock, predictable-sounding stuff. The guys and I would lay down a good rhythm track, which Henry would try to jazz up with a bunch of studio horn players doing schlock arrangements. It was torture. But what really galled us was that Morris could be so shortsighted and greedy, that he would use us this way just to turn a fast buck with his publishing. In fairness, Morris wasn't doing anything a hundred other record labels weren't doing, but that didn't make it go down any easier.

The only high point that week was receiving our first two gold records. The "Hanky Panky" single had sold nearly three million copies and the album had sold more than a million. We all went to Morris's office to take pictures for the trades. As we stood there holding our gold and smiling for the camera I remember thinking, "Enjoy it guys, because if this second album does not change direction fast, this may be as close to gold as we ever get again." As we were leaving Morris's office with the records under our arms we heard the voice. "Hey, where do you think you're going with those fucking things? They stay here."

On my way out, I went to Red's office for some consoling and to talk about the problems with the new album. Red was busy, so to kill time I began talking to Ronnie, his secretary. I'd had my eye on her for a while. She was three years older than I was, very sophisticated and very New York. I don't know what possessed me. Maybe it was the pixie hairdo, or the fact that I was just down and feeling lonely, but I asked her if she wanted to go out that night. She looked at me like I was from Mars. "You know there's a strict rule about secretaries going out with artists. I could lose my job." Really, I said? But then she smiled and said under her breath, "I live at 888 Eighth Avenue. Come over about eight." At least it wouldn't be hard to remember.

The 888 building was only a couple of blocks from the City Squire, and at eight sharp I rang the bell. When Ronnie opened the door and said, "Hi, come in," I knew I was crossing a threshold into dangerous territory. I was a married man and had no business being there. But she was beautiful and with the bliss of a sleepwalker, I crossed the line.

Her place turned out to be a small studio apartment that she shared with another girl. There were a few sticks of furniture, a couple of rollaway beds, and a record player. Ronnie told me to make myself at home while she finished dressing. Of course I went straight to the record player and started flipping through her stack of 45s, and I was surprised to come across an acetate demo. The title was "Hold on to Him" and the flip side was "World Down on Your Knees."

I asked Ronnie what the story was with this demo and she told me it was something her roommate's boyfriend had done. He was a songwriter at Kama Sutra named Ritchie Cordell.

I put it on the turntable and it was great. In fact, it sounded like a smash. I played the flip and that sounded great too. It was the best new stuff I had heard in months. "Damn, this is great," I said. "Can I do these songs?"

"I don't know," she said. "Do you want to talk to Ritchie? He'd love to meet you."

That night, Ronnie and I did the town. We went to all the hot rock clubs: Trudy Heller's, Max's Kansas City, the Phone

89

Booth, the Scene, even the Latin Quarter. We took taxis every-where. Somehow between Ronnie and the lights of the city I felt like I was in a Fred Astaire movie. Everything seemed terribly elegant and exciting. We made plans to do the same thing the next evening.

The following night I arrived at Ronnie's apartment and was welcomed by her roommate, Linda, and that was when I first laid eyes on Ritchie Cordell. What a character. He was a cross between Dr. Zorba and Harpo Marx, with granny glasses he wore on the tip of his nose that made his eyes look four times their normal size. We hit it off right away. Within twenty min-utes, we'd talked about everything, music, politics, science . . . I really liked the guy. I also told him I loved his songs and that I wanted to do "Hold on to Him." He said we should get together to write, and that I should meet his writing partner, Sal Trama-chi, that "Hold on to Him" was already a couple of months old and that I should hear their new stuff. He was very animated and very serious.

While we were talking, I could not help noticing that Ritchie had nonchalantly pulled out a vial of pot from his leather bag and started to roll a joint. Everybody else in the room seemed to think this was perfectly normal behavior. I had never smoked pot in my life and was getting nervous, and they all seemed to know it. I guess I still had a hayseed in my mouth. Ritchie casu-ally lit the joint, took a deep drag, and passed it to Linda, who took a deep drag and passed it to Ronnie, who took a deep drag and passed it to me. They were all staring at me and giggling. I slowly put the joint to my lips and took a puff. I held in the smoke for as long as I could and blew it out. Nothing. I took another puff and held it longer. I blew it out. Nothing. By now Ritchie and the girls were laughing. I had no idea what was so funny. I took another puff and held it until I almost passed out, then blew the smoke into the air. I was not sure what was supposed to happen but whatever it was, it wasn't. Then I turned to Ronnie and asked her if she had a beer. With this they all went into convulsions.

Finally I grabbed Ronnie's hand and we headed for the door. Ritchie, in between coughs and fits of laughter, said he would be up to see me tomorrow at Roulette. Ronnie and I had another big New York night. This would become a pattern. Every night I was not in the studio, I was with Ronnie. No doubt about it, we were falling in love and this was going to complicate things.

The next day Ritchie brought Sal Tramachi up to Roulette and we all met in Henry's office. Sal was skinny, about five foot seven, and very theatrical. He was so hyper he made Ritchie look calm by comparison. They played me about a dozen demos they had recently made: they had great hooks, great melodies, and I liked them all. I thought one in particular, "It's Only Love," really sounded like a hit. I was so excited, I immediately took them down to meet Morris. We walked in and I introduced them. I told Morris that these guys had a batch of new songs and I wanted to work with them.

Morris stood up like Caesar in the senate as if to say, "I'll take it from here." He glared at Ritchie and Sal and said, "Who are you guys signed with?" "Kama Sutra," they said. Morris yelled out the door, "KAREN, get me Artie Ripp." The three of us just looked at one another and it did not take long before Karen yelled back, "Artie's on line three." Morris pushed a button on the speakerphone so we could all hear. "How are you, bubbe? Listen, I got two of your writers up here. My artist wants to work with them." Morris and Artie talked some mumbo jumbo about publishing rights for a minute until Artie finally said, "Whatever you want, Moshe."

That was it. We were apparently going to be one big, happy

family. When the meeting with Morris was over, I felt a thousand pounds lighter. A few days later we were all in the studio recording "It's Only Love." But this time the atmosphere was great. We used the demo as a blueprint and everything clicked. We finished the record in less than three hours. Even Morris loved it and agreed that "It's Only Love" should be the next single. Ritchie and Sal had really pulled this one out for me, and I knew I wanted these guys permanently.

It was right around this time that Bob Mack, who had not been heard from in nearly two months, made an unexpected appearance at Roulette. Technically, he was still my manager, and he came to see Morris in the hopes of getting more money. Even I had to laugh at that one. Morris detested Mack. I hid with Red in his office and waited for the explosion. We were not disappointed. The meeting lasted three minutes and Morris went nuts. He wasted few words on Mack other than obscenities and instead picked him off his feet by his collar and smashed him against the wall of the office. "You're fucking with my artist." The sound was horrible. He threw Mack toward the door and Mack kept on walking, fast.

Even though I had my own bones to pick with Mack, he did not deserve that. After all, if it hadn't been for Mack, there wouldn't have been "Hanky Panky," or Tommy James for that matter. I owed him a lot. As he walked by me he was visibly shaken and pale. Hell, he was scared for his life. I stopped him and asked, "Are you all right?" All he said was "I'll call you later." That was the last time I ever laid eyes on him. I went into Morris's office. "What happened?" "You don't need that fucking guy," said Morris. "Well, what am I going to do for a manager?" I said. "You want a manager? I'll get you a fucking manager. KAREN, get me Lenny Stogel."

Who the hell was Lenny Stogel? I had to be very careful

around Morris because he took everything I said very seriously and he reacted instantly whether I wanted him to or not. He fixed problems I did not know I had, problems I did not necessarily want fixed. Every time Morris yelled "KAREN!" my life changed. In two minutes, Lenny Stogel was on line three. "Hey, bubbe, how are you? Got something for you."

In the ten minutes they talked, Morris told Lenny my life story and strongly suggested how great it would be for all of us if Lenny took me on as a client. He hung up the phone and told me I had a 2:00 appointment with Lenny the following afternoon at his apartment. "Don't be late."

Lenny Stogel, as it turned out, was a young, up-and-coming whiz kid in the industry who, at the time, managed Sam the Sham and the Pharaohs, the Royal Guardsmen, and several other acts. He was also married to Harry Fox's daughter. Harry Fox was the guy who collected the worldwide publishing royalties for nearly everyone in the music business. No wonder Morris liked Lenny so much. At 2:00 the following day, I was knocking on Lenny's apartment door.

Lenny lived in a gorgeous penthouse on the East Side of Manhattan, and for a thirty-two-year-old guy, he was doing okay. He gave me one of the best song-and-dance sales pitches I ever heard: the best venues, the biggest TV shows, never-ending publicity. If even half of what he said actually happened, my life was going to be pretty amazing. And even more incredible was that he was moving his whole operation into Ronnie's building at 888 Eighth Avenue. If that wasn't a sign, what was?

We shook hands and I had a new management team. Ironically, that week, Morris found out about me and Ronnie and fired her. We were both pretty upset about it but we knew we were playing with fire and breaking company policy. There wasn't much I could say to Morris as an excuse so I didn't say anything and neither did he. I am not sure what I was thinking but in the craziness of the moment, between being glad we did not have to hide anymore and feeling guilty for getting her fired, I did what I thought seemed right. I got my own apartment at 888 Eighth Avenue and Ronnie moved in with me. It was a one-bedroom efficiency on the eleventh floor, but after three months at the City Squire it felt like a suite at the Ritz. Ronnie fixed it up great with real plush carpeting, a mirrored wall, and new furniture from Maurice Valency.

That same week, Lenny Stogel and Associates took over most of the fifth floor at 888. The day he moved in, I went right down to see his new offices and to meet my whole management team who, up until then, had been nameless faces and were now all finally under one roof. Zac Glickman, Lenny's partner, handled the day-to-day operations with an amazing amount of poise considering he was only twenty-two years old. Janis Murray, a very soft-spoken woman with short, curly black hair, handled public relations and media. But most impressive to me was Herb Rosen, a funny-as-hell, fast-talking promotion man who owned New York radio. In fact, he was the greatest independent promo guy I ever saw. He was already a legend in New York and Lenny hired him to work all the Stogel and Associates acts. Herb and I developed a close friendship. He worked every one of my records in New York from that point on, and New York was the toughest market in the country. Red loved him and Herb became an integral part of our record success.

Even though the second album was not finished yet, Roulette had gone ahead and released "It's Only Love" as our third single, and it was starting to break. Morris was on Lenny's back to finish the album now! Lenny called me down to his office for an emergency strategy meeting. We decided the fastest way to get this album out was to combine the new stuff we had cut with some of the throwaway songs from the *Hanky Panky* album. All we needed was a cover photo.

Zac told us about a young female photographer up on the seventeenth floor in our building. Her name was Linda Eastman and she was extremely talented but not very experienced. He thought she was worth a try. Zac made the appointment and the next day the Shondells and I went up to her studio. The place was almost empty except for a few photos on the walls, pictures she had taken, mostly of rock and rollers. There were some props scattered about and a huge ceiling-to-floor, translucent screen with a slide projector behind it. She was very friendly but nervous. She told us this was her first studio session. Instead of making us apprehensive, her honesty and frankness reassured us. The whole shoot took less than an hour. When we saw the pictures a few days later, we were amazed at how good they were. We picked one shot and used it for the "It's Only Love" cover. Years later, when Linda Eastman McCartney, wife of Paul McCartney, published her award-winning compendium of her career in photography, she mentioned that Tommy James and the Shondells gave her her first professional job and featured the picture.

Two weeks later, the album was in the stores. Before we could catch our breath, Lenny hit us with a barrage of appearances we had to make, starting with the Dick Clark show *Where the Action Is,* in L.A. We flew out the night before the taping and stayed at the infamous "Riot House," the Hyatt House on Sunset Strip. This was our first trip to the West Coast and our first network TV show. We were very excited to be on television and even more thrilled about meeting Dick Clark.

The next morning we got up, jumped into a couple of cabs, and made our way over to Dick Clark Productions to catch a chartered bus out to Malibu, where the show was being taped. Somehow we got the departure time confused and missed the bus. We were frantic. Now we had to get both cabdrivers to take us all the way out to Malibu Beach and somehow find the location.

About two hours and six hundred dollars later, we found the spot, and the producer was pretty upset with us. After a brow-beating lecture about "time is money, kid" and the finer points of professionalism plus a lot of groveling from us, we were for-given, absolved, and allowed to meet Dick Clark, who could not have been nicer. We had a great talk while the other acts were performing. It turned out Dick was friends with Red Schwartz from the old days back in Philly, and he had been following my career from the start. I felt very honored that he took this much time with me.

We were on with Paul Revere and the Raiders, Tommy Roe, and the Cyrcle.

It was amazing watching the Raiders do their celebrated gui-tar fight. The lead guitarist and the bass player would swing the necks of their guitars over each other's heads, just barely miss-ing, as they each ducked in the nick of time to the beat of the music. Man, were we impressed. The show came off great, and the next day we were flying to Bermuda to play a weeklong gig at a place called the Forty Thieves Club in Hamilton.

When we landed in Bermuda, we were sort of half expect-ing a reception at the airport. Nothing big, mind you, just a few screaming girls or maybe a small press conference. After all, we were working on our third million-selling single. Nothing. No reporters. No radio stations. Not even an autograph hound. We hung around the baggage claim area posing conspicuously for photographers that would never come, waiting for a limousine and chauffeur that would never arrive. Finally, a cabdriver came over and said, "You go dis way, mon?" So the six of us with our luggage and equipment crammed into two broken-down Volkswagen Beetles and putt-putted our way to the Forty Thieves for a sound check.

The Forty Thieves turned out to be a hole in the wall that looked like half the bars in Niles, Michigan. Each table had a candle in a glass goblet covered with plastic fishnet. There was a linoleum dance floor about ten feet square. Lenny Stogel must have called in some favors to get us booked here. My God, I played better joints with Larry Coverdale. But then we noticed dozens of pictures of big-name celebrities who had played there lining the walls: musicians, comedians, and singers. Apparently this was where the action was in Bermuda.

During the sound check, we decided that if we wanted to try something new, this was the place. A guitar fight, like Paul Revere and the Raiders did. Who the hell would know? We figured we could insert it in the middle of a new song we were working on: "Land of 1000 Dances" by Cannibal and the Headhunters. We'd rehearsed it already and it seemed to work. Mike started by swinging the neck of his bass over Joe's head. Then Joe swung his guitar over Mike's head while I stood in between and ducked under both of them. All of us kept popping up and down like pistons in time to the music. We all knew this would be great.

By 8:00 that night, the place was packed. There were more than a thousand people in this little joint and it was an exotic mixture of locals and tourists. There was no one under thirty years old, not the kind of crowd we were used to.

From the dressing room, we could see our opening act on stage: four old island guys playing things they must have found in their backyards. One guy played a gutbucket bass, a broom handle with a single string connected to an upside-down bucket; another guy played a washboard with thimbles on his fingers;

the third played a cigar box with prongs. The only store-bought instrument was a slide whistle. And if that wasn't scary enough, the crowd loved them. We knew this could go either way: they would love us or hate us. The MC was an island guy in a Hawaiian shirt. He was half-loaded. "Here day are . . . Toddy Janes and de Shondell."

We hit the stage to nominal applause, and we had already decided to go full tilt fast. Don't give them time to think. We played our first three songs back to back to back. There was scattered clapping but nothing like what we were used to. This was going to be a tough crowd. We barely took a breath and went right into "Land of 1000 Dances." If the guitar fight didn't get them, nothing would. About halfway through the guitar solo, I signaled to Mike, who then signaled to Joe. The bell had rung and round one was on. Mike swung the neck of his bass over Joe's head while we both ducked. Joe bounced up and swung his guitar over Mike's head as Mike went down. The audience suddenly got excited. We did it again and now the audience was really into it. We were going great. Suddenly I heard a thump and a groan. As I looked up, I saw something flying through the air away from the stage. Mike's tuning peg had gotten caught in Joe's toupee and flung it out into the crowd, where it landed on a table, on top of one of those fishnet candles, and burst into flames. I looked back at Joe and there he stood, frozen like a snowball and just as bald, watching his wig burn. I had not even known he wore a toupee. Somebody grabbed a fire extinguisher and doused the burning rug, finally stomping it out on the floor. The crowd went crazy. They thought it was part of the act. We pretended it was and somehow got through the set. Afterward, the club owner came up to us and said, "You guys were great. Do you do that thing with the hair every night?" "No," we said. "Just the first night. It sort of creates a buzz."

* * *

As soon as we got back from Bermuda, Ritchie Cordell and I had a meeting in Henry Glover's office. That was the day I met Bo Gentry. Bo, like Ritchie, had been a staff writer and producer for Artie Ripp at Kama Sutra. Because of a recent falling-out with Artie, Bo was now unemployed, and Ritchie had grabbed him, thinking he would be perfect for our new team. Bo was a wiry, cadaverous twenty-four-year-old musician with a real wise-ass attitude and a scathing, sometimes vicious sense of humor that complemented Ritchie's charming, mad scientist demeanor. Bo did not waste time on pleasantries but sat down at the piano. Ritchie grabbed my arm and said, "Listen to this. We've been working all night." Bo played single notes on the bass keys, an octave apart, while Ritchie sang:

> "Children behave . . .
> That's what they say when we're together."

And then they played me a hook that blew me away.

> "I think we're alone now.
> There doesn't seem to be anyone around."

No matter how badly Bo played the piano, no matter how off-key Ritchie sang, this was a smash. They played it again, and again and I liked it more every time. "You guys wait here." I ran to Morris's office. He was on the phone but he hung up and waved me right in. "So what's up, kid? You got the next single?" "Morris," I said, "Ritchie and his new partner just played me a fucking number one record." "Well, get them in here," said Morris.

I brought Ritchie and Bo into the office, and the first thing

Morris said was, "Who's got the publishing?" Bo said that he was still signed to Artie Ripp. "Fuck Artie Ripp," said Morris. "We'll put it in Ritchie's name."

So Ritchie and Bo made a private deal with Morris to split the royalties and we were in business. Ritchie booked time at Allegro Studios in the basement of 1650 Broadway. We met around noon and I was introduced to the owner and head engineer, Bruce Staple. This was a completely different world from Bell Sound Studios. The control booth looked like the console in a spaceship. Indirect light on the walls gave the place a futuristic feel, but above all, it had a hip, creative atmosphere that made everything look and sound great.

Bo sat down at a beautiful Baldwin grand piano that was miked in stereo. Ritchie sat behind the drums in a semienclosed, acoustic drum bay with each drum and cymbal separately miked and perfectly tuned. Next to the drum bay was a row of guitar and bass amplifiers with acoustic baffling between each. I picked my old favorite, an Ampeg Gemini II, and plugged in my Fender Jazzmaster guitar. We put on matching stereo headphones with separate volume controls and we were ready. I was not sure if the three of us together could play more than a dozen chords but we sure looked cool.

First we raised the key from G to A and then started toying with the arrangement. Ritchie and Bo originally wrote the song as a mid-tempo ballad. I said no way and started speeding it up. I began playing the staccato eighth notes on the bass strings just like Larry Coverdale and I did in the old days. Bo began pounding out quarter notes on the piano. Ritchie grabbed some drumsticks and did the best he could. I then put on a nasally, almost juvenile-sounding lead vocal, and without realizing it, we invented "bubblegum" music. Bruce threw together a rough mix on a 7½ -inch tape and Bo, Ritchie, and I ran the three blocks back to Roulette. We played it for Morris and Red Schwartz, and they both flipped out. Morris wound up playing it for everybody in the office, including the secretaries. The whole place went nuts for the song. At first, Morris wanted to release the demo as the single but we emphatically nixed that idea, and he refreshingly and surprisingly acquiesced. The following week, we booked time at Allegro to finish the record and make a master.

Henry Glover's secretary asked me if I wanted to hire an arranger or were we going to do everything ourselves? I thought a good arranger might not be a bad idea. The only name that came to me was Jimmy Wisner. I had seen his credits on a record I loved from the previous year, called "1–2–3" by Len Barry. Henry's secretary said, "No problem," and we met with Jimmy the following day at Roulette.

Jimmy turned out to be a very straight-laced, middle-aged professional. He was a sophisticated, well-schooled musician and loved the idea of highbrow arrangements over simple three-chord rock and roll. The Beatles may have had George Martin, but we had Jimmy. When we all met at Allegro the next week, we were astonished to find that Jimmy had booked a small symphony orchestra complete with cellos, chimes, and an ondioline. All I kept thinking was *What the hell am I going to tell Morris when he gets the bill for all this?*

Bo, Ritchie, and I went into the control booth and listened as the musicians ran it down for the first time. There was something almost comical about an orchestra playing this little ditty-bop tune as if it were Beethoven. It sounded great but it was too much, too big. We did about eight takes and sent the players home. We then sifted through this mountain of music in a process we went on to call "finding the record," which meant throwing out 90 percent of what we created until we found something we liked. We continually switched tracks on and off and in some spots we left nothing but the bass and drums. Two days later, on Christmas Eve 1966, I laid down the vocal track and, thank God, we had our record.

With what was to become my standard practice, I took the record up to Morris and handed it in like a schoolboy handing in a term paper. "Is that the next single? Let's hear what you got."

"I Think We're Alone Now" was released the first week of January 1967. Radio loved it and it exploded. Within two weeks, we had virtually every major station in the country playing the record. It climbed the charts steadily through February, March, and April in jumps of eight to ten points a week. From Roulette's point of view this was the perfect way to have a hit, slow and relentless. It ensured we would keep our bullet in the trade papers, which in turn kept radio playing the record, which in turn kept the record selling. This also gave us the time we needed to come up with a follow-up and put the album together. As usual, we had the hit before we had the album.

One night at Bo's apartment during a writing session, a tape of "I Think We're Alone Now" was accidentally put on the reel-to-reel upside down. When it was played, it came out backward. When we heard the chord progression in reverse, our jaws dropped. The song sounded just as good backward as it did forward. Ritchie jumped up and said, "That's great, let's write it."

Bo and Ritchie banged out a new set of lyrics and called the song "Mirage," which we recorded along with the rest of the album, using Jimmy Wisner's approach of overkill orchestration and our own technique of "finding the record," and on the heels of "I Think We're Alone Now," "Mirage" was quickly released as the follow-up single. In a glutinous feeding frenzy, Morris then put out a third single, "I Like the Way," a mere eight weeks later. This was an unheard-of release schedule, forcing radio on to the next single before the previous one peaked. Incredibly, they did it. All three singles went gold, and by June, the album went platinum.

The success of the *I Think We're Alone Now* album and the hit singles that came from it really changed us. Tommy James and the Shondells were no longer the garage band with the fluky hit. We now had a new sound that was uniquely ours. The tight rhythms and the staccato eighth notes that we pioneered and used throughout the album became our signature sound. Because of this, the band changed too. Not only was Morris not paying me, he wasn't even paying the band their promised weekly salary. This got to be such an issue that, one night, half my band went to the promoter before I did and took all the money. I could understand their frustration, but they should have come to me first and I would have done what I could to correct the problem. Later that week, because of the way they handled this situation and because there now was so much bad feeling that it had created two separate camps, I had to fire Joe, George, and Vinnie. What I thought was just Morris's negligence turned out to cause a severe disruption in the band. Thank God we found Pete Lucia on drums and Eddie Gray on guitar to come on board and pick up the slack. Tommy James and the Shondells was now a crisp five-piece guitar-oriented pop band. There were other changes too.

Somewhere during the frenzy of recording, we all started popping pills. Amphetamines, to be exact. Somebody always seemed to have a pocket full of them, but I was the worst offender. By the end of the album, the control booth looked like a pharmacy. There were yellow ones before doing the lead vocals; blue and pink ones to help us write. Dexedrine, Eskatrol, black beauties,

Desbutal, and on and on. No wonder we were crisp. The pills and the grinding schedule just seemed to work together. And when you are nineteen years old, you think you are indestructible.

Morris, by the way, was the happiest I had even seen him. Roulette had not had a creative team like this since the George Goldner–Alan Freed glory days of the late fifties. Things were really humming until one day, in late May, a squadron of IRS agents paid Morris a visit. It seems there was something not quite kosher about Morris's books and they were there to get to the bottom of it. Morris treated them with the same contempt he had for every other authority figure and told them, "Get the fuck out of my office." They were turned over to poor, beleaguered Howard Fisher. We all took bets on which of the twelve sets of books he was going to show them. The IRS boys would continue on their expedition to nowhere for the next two and a half years.

CHAPTER FIVE

Gettin' Together

In the spring of 1967, just before the Summer of Love would embrace America, the Shondells and I were riding high. "I Think We're Alone Now" was our fourth monster hit and it seemed like it stayed on the charts forever. That was followed by "Mirage" in April, while "I Like the Way" was getting ready for release and would also go gold. But we were ecstatic when we learned another of the songs from the album, "(Baby, Baby) I Can't Take It No More," would be our first song to be covered by another artist, an R&B singer named Verdelle Smith on Capitol Records. When I first heard the record I was thrilled, of course, but I also felt strangely self-conscious and even a little embarrassed, but nothing else says you've arrived more than someone else covering one of your songs. There was some silliness as well. It seems incredible now, but there was some initial resistance to "I Think We're Alone Now." A lot of radio DJs and programmers thought it was dirty. We even had to change the cover of the *I Think We're Alone Now* album because it showed a boy's and girl's bare footprints in the sand going off together into the distance side by side until they turn and face each other in a way that seemed very suggestive. And this, at a time when the Rolling Stones had the number one record in the country with "Let's Spend the Night Together." Red worked very hard to smooth all the ruffled feathers and eventually wore down the opposition.

We toured everywhere that year, which was great because we made money. It was the only part of the financial arrangement that Morris seemed to have no control over. I guess he was content with his near monopoly on record sales, royalties, and publishing. Early in May, which was sort of a prelude to our big summer tour, we did a gig at the Steel Pier in Atlantic City. I rode down in a limousine to meet the band, who were coming in from Pittsburgh. The whole idea of the boardwalk just blew me away. Even though school hadn't let out yet, there were thousands of people walking or riding on jitneys up and down the boardwalk, munching on cheese dogs and chewing saltwater taffy. It was like seeing the Monopoly board game come to life. They had nothing like this in Michigan. We pulled up to the Steel Pier by a colossal pavilion with a gigantic marquee that you could have seen a mile away. The lettering was huge, nearly twenty feet tall, and it said RICK NELSON AND TOMMY JAMES! (After Ricky turned twenty-one in 1961, he was always billed as "Rick.") Ricky had always been a special hero of mine because he was part of the first generation of rockers, he'd been a TV star ever since he was six years old, and I loved his music.

There were two venues at the Steel Pier. Ricky was playing the theater, which was an older crowd, and we were performing in a large geodesic dome, another gigantic concert space at the end of the pier for the younger set. We had to walk all the way around this dome to get to the back of the stage. There was no back entrance so we were led around the crowd by security guards while all the kids screamed and cheered. The opening act was already on stage. It was an instrumental group, and as I listened to the music, it sounded like a small big band with a nice-sized horn section. The one thing I noticed before I got backstage was that the drummer was in a sharp-looking, iridescent gray sports coat and that he was dressed differently from the band. By the time we got to the dressing rooms, they were just finishing.

In the dressing room, we started to change clothes and get ready for the show. As I was talking to the promoter, I felt hot and stuffy so I decided to open a little window to get some fresh air. The window opened onto a cement terrace with a large water tank and a big bleacher section jammed with people, where still more entertainment was going on. I might as well have opened a porthole. Just as I raised the window, a gush of water, about ten gallons, came through, splashing me and drenching the dressing room floor. This was my introduction to the diving horse, which went on between the acts to keep the crowd entertained. The dressing room looked like it had been hit by a tsunami.

After everybody dried off, we started out toward the stage, but first I wanted to meet the opening act, which was something I always tried to do. One of the stage managers took me over to their dressing room, and as I walked in I could see, asleep on two straight-back folding chairs, the gray-haired drummer who was still in his shiny suit. I realized it was Gene Krupa, Benny Goodman's old drummer from the glory years of the swing era. During the 1930s and '40s, he was the most famous drummer in the world. Without realizing it, I was on the same bill with two of my heroes, even though one of them looked like a fallen hero. When I looked at the stage manager, he just shrugged his shoulders and made a motion with his hand as if he were shooting a needle into his arm. "He stays passed out like this until they wake him up for the next show." It seemed even the musicians from my parents' generation had their drug of choice: heroin. Thank God, I didn't fool around with that stuff. Of course, I then popped two black beauties and the Shondells and I went on stage.

At some point during the gig, I had a great talk with Ricky Nelson. Our conversation was essentially me gushing about what a big fan I was and how I had always loved his music and that my first public performance ever was "Lonesome Town" before my high school class back in Niles when I was twelve years old. In fact, it was what got me to organize my first group, which eventually became the Shondells. He was dressed in a khaki three-piece suit and was very conservative, in that quiet way he always had on TV. The music business was so different since he'd first broke out in 1957, and he hadn't had a big hit in a couple of years. He had not yet reinvented himself as the "Garden Party" Rick Nelson. I was flabbergasted when he told me he liked my music. I don't know how impressed he was, but it was important to me that I told him how much he meant to me.

We worked with another of my heroes that summer. In Boston, we played with the Beach Boys at the Back Bay Theater and I was so blown away not just by them but by their stage gear. We had never worked with a professional monitor system before. They had a truck for nothing but their front sound system and monitors. We were still using whatever contraption the venue handed us, shouting into the microphones and hoping the crowd could hear us. The Beach Boys had a guy out of New Jersey named Jersey Joe who ran their sound. They were just coming off their hit single "Good Vibrations" so they were also riding high. It was amazing watching them perform, especially Mike Love on the theremin. It sounded like you were in a studio. We got to use their system because we were sharing the stage and everything was set up for them. That turned our heads around, and we traveled with our own sound system from then on.

We also played with the Monkees that year at a lot of ball-parks. The one I remember best was the new Atlanta Braves ballpark. The 1910 Fruitgum Co. opened the show. We were the middle act. At that time the Monkees were working for the unheard-of amount of $100,000 guaranteed or 100 per-cent of the gate, which was a deal nobody was getting. Even the Stones and the Beatles didn't have that kind of deal. The promoter made nothing, but he looked like a hero and prob-ably thought that would cement his reputation. I don't even think he recouped his losses. We got paid, but in essence, every-body was working for the Monkees. At that moment, the Mon-kees were the biggest act imaginable. They were having Top 10 hits, they had a hit TV show, and they were every American teenybopper's heartthrobs. We played with them a few more times in '67, including a concert at the newly built Astrodome in Houston, Texas. Another thing that happened after "I Think We're Alone Now" was that the industry treated us differently. Radio, magazines, and television all treated us with a lot more respect than when we were the kids who had had this one hit out of Pittsburgh. Red Schwartz, who I spoke with every day no matter where we were or what we were doing, was able to get the top jocks and program directors on the phone anytime, day or night, with news about Tommy James. And the band and I were seeing ourselves differently. One day I woke up and I became a New Yorker. I think it hit me when I went home for a short visit and all my relatives sounded like hillbillies. When you think your mom and dad have accents, you know some-thing has changed. New York looked normal.

I was getting acclimated to the city through Ronnie and just being in the center of this great creative merry-go-round called the music business. It was more than hitting the nightspots and buying new clothes. I was actually able to hail a cab by myself and know how to tip a waiter without getting glared at like a tourist. If it wasn't for Ronnie I would have stayed hidden in my hotel room. Ronnie got me out of my gopher hole. Back in Niles, I was the musical prodigy and nearly everybody else in my world was tone deaf. But in New York, everybody was as musically good as or better than I was. That was a great spur to get not only me but the other Shondells to keep thinking creatively. We would argue and debate in what direction the band should go. Getting to know other bands was a revelation. When I used to stop by the Brill Building, I was always amazed at how Otis Blackwell or Jay and the Americans ran their musical operation like a well-oiled business. I had grown mildly savvy in Niles but it was nothing compared to what these guys were doing. And because pop music was changing so fast, we were always aware of our competition and what move we would need to make next.

We really grew into seasoned professionals in 1967 by insisting on "rock star" treatment. We were playing consistently for crowds of 50,000 and 60,000 people, and we were beginning to understand what it meant to be stars, which was great fun. Since we'd started at Roulette, we'd always found ourselves staying at the Holiday Inn in order to save the promoters and our manager money. Nobody figured out that we should be staying at the Hilton or the Sheraton. We would blow into town like heroes and there would be a big sign on the marquee of the Holiday Inn saying: WELCOME TOMMY JAMES AND THE SHONDELLS. It was usually above another announcement like: WELCOME SCHWARTZ BAR MITZVAH or ALL YOU CAN EAT FISH-FRY. We must have stayed at every Holiday Inn in the country. I think it was something Lenny Stogel arranged. Sometimes we had to double up and share beds. One night, we were so exhausted that Ronnie Rosman and I, half-asleep, must have thought we were home with our wives or girlfriends and started to put our arms around each other. The two of us woke up, screamed, and nearly fell off the bed. That was it. We were "stars" now, and that year we insisted on better treatment.

First, we invested in an official Tommy James and the Shondells truck with our name painted on the sides, which, of course, was like a neon sign saying "Please steal our stuff." Next, we gave the green station wagon an honorable retirement and began riding around in limousines, and then we hired roadies to do the heavy lifting. Nineteen sixty-seven was the year we upgraded.

Through all the traveling and one-night stands, I was constantly returning to New York to do publicity and work on the next album. In May 1967, I met with Bo and Ritchie at Bo's apartment on Fifty-first Street between Eighth and Ninth avenues to talk about our next project. Bo had become a hippie by this time and had completely embraced the flower child look, even if he still acted like a street punk. He had acquired what could only be called "homeless chic," which was kind of popular back then. He had holes in his jeans; he wore construction boots without socks, and carried around a leather shoulder bag with lots of fringe. His apartment was filled with overstuffed pillows and all the doorjambs had hanging beads. There were posters of naked girls on the walls that became transformed under the glow of a black light and the whole place smelled like pot and incense. He might have even had a lava lamp. We lit the customary joint and I settled down to listen to whatever new material they were working on. Bo played some things for me on his upright piano, but nothing sounded good and it wasn't because his keyboard was constantly out of tune. While Bo was playing, I noticed an acetate record out of its cover, titled "Gettin' Together" with Gene Pitney's name on it. I picked it up and

111

said, "What's this?" "Something I'm working on." I could tell I had touched a nerve. He did not want to talk about it and there was tension in the room. There was always tension when I was with Bo and Ritchie, that's just the way they were, but this was different. I made them play it for me. I looked directly at Bo after the record was over and he said, "It's just something I did." "Can I do it?" Silence. "Let me ask you something," I said. "Why wasn't I shown this? Why wasn't I given the right of first refusal?" Bo gave a bogus answer but I could see he knew this wasn't going to end well. I didn't want to hear anymore. "I like this a lot," I said, "and I'm doing this."

I went right to Roulette and walked into Morris's office and I told him how upset I was with Bo, that he had this record I liked but that he went behind my back and recorded it with Gene Pitney. "Fuck Gene Pitney," said Morris and he called Bo. "Get over here right now and bring that record Tommy likes." A half hour later we were all in Morris's office listening to Gene Pitney sing my next single. Ritchie could not have cared less, but I could see that Bo was mad, probably because he knew there was nothing he could do about it. "Fuck Gene Pitney." That's all it took. End of story. "Gettin' Together" turned out to be our seventh gold record and I always felt like I owed Gene Pitney an apology.

I suppose it's best to clarify a few things. It is always reported that there are five major crime families in New York—Gambino, Genovese, Colombo, Lucchese, and Bonanno—and that's mostly true. But back in the sixties, there were six families. All of the above and the Roulette family. It was not for nothing that Morris Levy was called the Godfather of the music business. People from all over the industry called him or came to him to sort out problems. If somebody from Atlantic Records or Kama

Sutra found out that their records were being bootlegged, they called Morris. It seemed like once a month Morris would grab Nate McCalla and a few baseball bats, which were always in his office, and take off for somewhere in New Jersey or upstate New York. It was a ritual. "KAREN," he would yell out to his secretary, baseball bat in hand. "Call my lawyer." And off they would go.

Herb Rosen told me about an encounter with a bootlegger he got from Nate himself. Morris got a call from one of the big record labels that someone was bootlegging the company's records. They had an address in Brooklyn, so Morris and Nate grabbed their bats and were off to Flatbush. They broke into the building and found one guy busy pressing records. They tied the terrified guy to a chair, smashed the machinery, and then piled the records around him and doused them with gasoline. Morris lit a match and asked the guy who was behind it all. The man was in tears, swearing that it was only him, that he was doing it all to pay for an operation for his kid. Morris blew out the match and said, "If you're lying, I'll kill you."

They left the building, threw the guy into the car, and drove to a nearby hospital. Sure enough, the man's child was in intensive care. Morris talked to the hospital officials, wrote out a check for the operation, and told the guy, "Don't ever do this again."

But Morris used more than just muscle, and he worked with everybody in the business. If someone needed a change in their contract, Morris would arrange a deal. If someone wanted to leave one company and go to another, Morris would handle the details. If someone needed money because they were broke or bankrupt, Morris would arrange the financing. If you wanted a song that Gene Pitney had already recorded, you went to Morris and Morris would fix it. Of course, you would then be in debt to Morris and that could mean anything from an IOU you took very seriously to buying bonds for Israel. Morris ran his business like a "family" business. He protected you, but he also demanded loyalty and a hell of a lot of money. He was constantly on the phone, making deals. I never saw a guy use the phone so much. Every time I would come to see him he would be on the phone making a publishing deal in Britain or chatting up Cardinal Spellman or organizing a dinner for the United Jewish Appeal, or just saying hello to James Brown or Bob Hope.

The most expendable commodity in Morris's world was songwriters, who he probably felt were immediately replaceable. The big joke at Roulette was that scientists were trying to find the quietest place on earth. Answer: the Royalty Department at Roulette. Howard Fisher, who issued the checks, was the most harassed man I ever met. It seemed at some point every songwriter, recording artist, producer, musician, and IRS agent in the country came banging at Howard's door. Karen told me that during the great blackout of 1965, no one at Roulette knew the problem extended from Canada to New Jersey. Everyone thought that Con Edison had just shut off all the power in the building. Everyone ran into Howard's office screaming, "For God's sake, pay the electric bill already!"

Oddly enough, a few royalty statements were paid out regularly. They were royalties owed to that famous songwriter Morris Levy. If you weren't careful, Morris's writing credits would appear on songs that were actually written and recorded months before the record was purchased by Roulette. Even Morris's son, Adam, was given the occasional writing credit, which was very odd because at the time Adam was busy attending kindergarten.

This was the reason Bo was so mad. Morris wasn't paying him, and Bo started getting an attitude. Just before June, I went into the studio by myself to do the lead vocal and harmonies for "Gettin' Together." Bo and Ritchie had gone in with Jimmy Wisner separately to put together the music track but the feeling had soured. Everybody was getting an attitude. I couldn't really dwell on it because I had to leave the next day to begin our big summer tour.

The summer tour of 1967 was really the first big tour in which the Shondells and I were involved. It had always been random one-nighters up to that point. This was a bus tour put together by Lenny Stogel and included all of his acts. Sam the Sham and the Pharaohs were the headliners, and the Royal Guardsmen opened the show. They had a crazy made-for-radio novelty hit earlier that year called "Snoopy vs. the Red Baron." And then came an act named simply Keith, who had a big hit called "98.6." We went on just before Sam. Sam was older than we were and he was a good guy. He had a good band. The last real solid hit he'd had was "Little Red Riding Hood" in 1966, and of course they scored big the year before with "Wooly Bully." They were popular beyond the number of hits they had partly because of their outlandish image, which was perfect for the times. Sam wore a turban and the female backup singers, the Shamettes, dressed in metallic skirts with slits down the side. The band wore puffy pirate shirts. Lenny booked the tour through William Morris and all the acts were handled by Lenny and his management team. I didn't want to ride on a bus for weeks at a time, and I had to keep returning to New York whenever we were not performing, so I hired a driver and a gold Cadillac, which, of course, endeared me to everyone on the bus. My driver's name was Vito, and he had a hard time controlling all the high-tech gadgets in the car, especially the power windows. I'd be talking to someone outside the car from inside and suddenly the window would be rolling up on my neck. "Sorry, Tommy," he would say.

We had a big tour kick-off party in Manhattan, and all the jocks from WMCA radio were there. WMCA was the 5,000-watt station up against WABC, which was the 50,000-watt station. The most popular jock at WMCA was Jack Specter. He had been hired as our traveling MC and went on the whole tour with us, which lasted about eight weeks. Jack made a sad kind of history years later, by actually dying on the air. We played all over the country, and it was the first time we were merchandised with shirts, tour books, and lots of prepress and promotion. I finished the tour, but just barely. My voice was cracked and sore. We were sometimes doing five shows a week in different cities, and the pills and cigarettes were starting to take their toll. I was starting to look bad, losing lots of weight. When there was downtime, I was going back and forth to see Ronnie in New York or making spot visits back to Niles to see my family. I would blow through Niles like a tornado, spending what time I could, arms filled with money and gifts.

While we were out on the road, Lenny Stogel and his wife, Myrna, discovered a great new group called the Cowsills while they were rehearsing on the family farm in Connecticut. The reason the band was so unique for rock and roll was that they were an actual family. The mother, brothers, and sister all performed while the father managed them. Lenny got them a deal with MGM, and Mike Curb, the golden boy, who at twenty-one years old became the president of the company, signed them. Artie Kornfeld, who would later go on to help create the Woodstock festival, produced them and wrote their first hit, "The Rain, the Park, and Other Things." In addition, Jimmy Wisner was brought in to do their arrangements.

Because of all the personal connections, I felt like I had a stake in this act. Every time I hear that first Cowsills hit, it evokes memories of that time and place. It was one of the greatest-sounding records I ever heard. It was as powerfully emotional and evocative as "Good Vibrations" by the Beach Boys. When the NBC network had such a great success with the Monkees TV show, ABC wanted to get into the act and they conceived a show based on and starring the Cowsills, but there was so much haggling with the father that the deal fell through and the musical actress Shirley Jones and her son David Cassidy went on to star in *The Partridge Family*, which was one of the highest-rated television shows in the early seventies. David Cassidy is still performing the hits from the TV show to this day.

Lenny started a new company called Heroic Age Publicity and had Janis Murray run it out of 888 Eighth Avenue. Most of the people in my professional life were all living at 888. It was one of the great show business buildings in New York. Lenny lived there and so did Zac, Linda Eastman, Jimmy Wisner, along with other celebrities like Laura Nyro and Howard Keal. Then the Cowsills moved in on the ground floor. It was one big happy family, except the father drank heavily. He was an ex-serviceman, a big, burly guy who would occasionally come home crocked and get violent with the kids. A couple of them would come up to my place and hang out until the dust settled and then go back downstairs. That happened several times. The Cowsills were regulars on *The Ed Sullivan Show* that year. He adored them. They were good kids and it really was a nice family when the old man was not drinking.

Many people point to 1968 as the pivotal year in rock, but the sea change actually occurred in 1967. One of the things I remember so clearly was that it was the beginning of psychedelic music and FM underground radio. The music was getting away from the AM Top 40 format. The songs were getting longer and the melodies and themes were moving away from traditional pop into something that didn't really have a name yet. Just after the breakup and reorganization of the band, I went up to Pittsburgh for a rehearsal. I decided we needed to revamp the show and make it fit our new sound and the smaller, tighter, five-piece group we now were. A couple of the Shondells picked me up at the airport and on the way to rehearsal I was blown away when I heard the new Beatles single, "Strawberry Fields." But what really stunned me was that the next song was "Happy Together" by the Turtles. The Turtles' song was a great pop AM radio hit while "Strawberry Fields" was something else. It belonged on FM underground radio, not Top 40 radio. That is when I realized a shift was occurring and it was not just in the music business. In 1967, the first whiff of Eastern influence really entered the general culture. People were taking up yoga and meditating, and even old-guard stars like Sammy Davis, Jr., started wearing Nehru jackets and medallions. Bellbottoms and beads became part of everyone's uniform. The new acts coming out that year, like Big Brother and the Holding Company with Janis Joplin on lead vocals, the Doors, the Jefferson Airplane, and Cream, all had an edge to their music. There was still a good-natured feeling about everything. Drugs were still just "recreational," and Vietnam had not yet turned into the mess it later became. The presidential elections were still a year off. It was that time in between pop and "heavy."

We were still doing teen magazine promotions, "Win a Date with Tommy," that kind of thing. But at the same time, we wanted underground airplay. We wanted to be taken seriously, and the only way to do that was to get on FM radio. Being pop was starting to become just a little bit uncool. I think a lot of the "pop" acts started feeling that way. You were always trying to prove you had hair in all the right places. It was as if your voice hadn't changed yet so everybody started growing mustaches

Tommy's dad and mom, Joe and Belle Jackson, on their honeymoon, 1937.

Tommy "Jackson" with his first guitar, 1957.

Fourteen-year-old Tommy with his first rock band, the Tornadoes.
Left to right: Mike Finch (sax), Nelson Shepard (drums),
TJ, Larry Wright (bass), Larry Coverdale (guitar), 1962.

Tommy in the Spin-It record shop, Niles, Michigan. Left to right: resident musicologist "Dr. John," store clerks Bobbie Mansfield and TJ with shop owner Edith "Dickie" Frucci, 1963.

The original Shondells: The group that recorded "Hanky Panky" on Snap Records. Left to right: Larry Wright (bass), Craig Villeneuve (piano), TJ, Jim Payne (drums), Larry Coverdale (guitar), 1964.

Tommy's first wife, Diane, and son, Brian, 1967.

Tommy and the Shondells being awarded their first gold record for "Hanky Panky" by Roulette Records president Morris Levy. Left to right: Ron Rosman, George Magura, TJ, Vinnie Pietropali, Mike Vale, Joe Kessler, Morris Levy, 1966.

Tommy signs an exclusive management agreement with Leonard Stogel and Associates in Morris Levy's office with Lenny and Morris looking on, 1966.

Writer-producer Ritchie Cordell and Tommy heading for the studio, 1967.

Christmas party at Morris Levy's nightclub the Round Table. Left to right: executive secretary of Amy/Mala/Bell Records Caroline Nikano; record company president Larry Utall; president of Calla Records and Morris's bodyguard, Nate McCalla; senior editor of *Record World* magazine Bob Austin; Morris Levy; Roulette's in-house lawyer, Normand Kurtz; and Morris's personal secretary, Karen Grasso, 1967.

Manhattan's famous Mutual of New York building that inspired Tommy's smash hit "Mony Mony," 1968.

Tommy and the Shondells on their first *Ed Sullivan Show* appearance. Left to right: Ed Sullivan, TJ, Ron Rosman (keyboards), Mike Vale (bass), Pete Lucia (drums), Eddie Gray (guitar), 1969.

THE ROULETTE REGULARS

Gaetano "Corky" Vastola was a close associate of Morris Levy. He was an underboss for the DeCavalcante family, the New Jersey wing of the Genovese family. Vastola was one of the principle owners of Roulette and was often seen with Morris discussing record company business. Ironically, one of the numerous crimes that later sent Gambino family crime boss John Gotti to prison for life was his planned hit on Vastola, whom he regarded as a stool pigeon. Vastola was ultimately convicted along with Morris in 1988 for the brutal beating and extortion of Philadelphia record retailer John LaMonte and sentenced to twenty years in prison. Morris died, however, before serving a day.

Morris Levy's business partner and Genovese crime family head Thomas "Tommy Ryan" Eboli. Acting boss under imprisoned Don Vito Genovese, 1960–1969. Made "official successor" after Genovese's death in '69. Assassinated in 1972.

Dominick "Quiet Dom" Cirillo, one of Morris Levy's associates and a Roulette regular. He originally served as a messenger between Vito Genovese and the rest of the family and later became acting boss, 1997–1998.

Anthony "Fat Tony" Salerno, Morris Levy's friend and cohort, looked after the Genovese family interests in New Jersey and later became family head, 1981–1986. "Fat Tony" was the primary model for Tony Soprano in TV's *The Sopranos,* while Morris "Moish" Levy was the model for record promoter Hesh Rabkin on the same show.

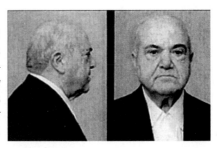

Vincent "the Chin" Gigante took over as family head in 1986 after "Fat Tony" Salerno's hundred-year sentence for racketeering and held the reins in prison until his death in 2005, the longest run in Genovese history. Before he was known as the ultimate crime boss, he was a capo and considered a major up-and-comer in the family. He is seen here in 1957, shortly after his arrest for an attempted hit on family head Frank Costello. The stage manager of that affair was none other than Morris Levy's partner Tommy Eboli, who recruited Gigante for the hit and drove the getaway car.

Tommy and his second wife, Ronnie, arriving in Hawaii, 1969.

Morris Levy presenting Tommy with a gold record for *Crimson and Clover,* 1969.

Morris Levy and his son Adam at Morris's farm in upstate New York, 1973.

"Fat Tony" Salerno in a gentler moment helping Morris's son Adam with his winter jacket up at Morris's farm.

Former vice president Hubert H. Humphrey presenting Tommy with a State Department award, 1975.

Roulette's national promotion director Red Schwartz and Tommy, 1987.

Aegis Records president Ron Alexenburg, Tommy, TJ's manager Carol Ross Durborow, and Aegis Records executive Joe Cohen, 1990.

Tommy and producer-arranger Jimmy Wisner in the studio listening to a final mix, 1995.

Tommy and Lynda James, 1990.

Tommy James today.

and stopped cutting their hair. It was important to start looking scruffy. The scruffier the better. When the Beatles came out with *Sgt. Pepper's Lonely Hearts Club Band,* that iced it. That was the dividing line. But it was also true that not all the kids were ready for the new sounds like acid rock and hard blues–rock and the psychedelic stuff.

This music scared the shit out of me. It was radically different from what we were doing. It was intimidating, and we weren't sure we were going to be able to fit in. AM radio played our records alongside the more avant-garde stuff and they didn't seem to notice the difference, but I did. When I heard "Gettin' Together" next to "White Room" by Cream, I knew the formula was changing. Absurdly, while this great change in musical styles was occurring, bubblegum music was also being invented.

In its own weird way, bubblegum was a kind of prepunk rock and roll. That summer, every time I went up to see Morris there were two guys sitting in the waiting room: Jerry Kasenetz and Jeff Katz. They were two young record producers who were trying to get Morris to invest in them, and for whatever reason Morris was avoiding them. I would pass these guys, say hello, and walk right into Morris's office as usual. I think it may have annoyed them. But I never made an appointment to see Morris. Unless the doors were closed and Morris was meeting with "the boys," his office was my office. After about six months of getting the cold shoulder from Morris, Kasenetz and Katz signed with Laurie Records and grabbed a jingles singer named Joey Levine to do lead vocals. Jeff and Jerry went on to make their prefab rock and roll. The term *Bubblegum* was used to describe one of their first groups, the 1910 Fruitgum Company. It was cute and accurate, and we didn't pay too much attention to it until it became clear they were bastardizing the intro of "I Think We're Alone Now" and "Mirage," causing us to get stuck

119

with the label too. Then we started to resent it, as if we had created it. No one ever called "I Think We're Alone Now" bubble-gum before that.

Most people today will deny liking it, but it sold like crazy, so somebody must have been buying it. Jeff and Jerry went on to create Ohio Express and their many offshoots, like the Archies, who actually were cartoon characters. Jeff and Jerry made a fortune but for some reason Morris could not have cared less that he let them slip away. Maybe he felt he didn't need another writing team that he wasn't going to pay anyway.

Throughout the summer, we played other gigs beyond the bus-stop tour with Sam the Sham. One show was in Phoenix at a band shell in the city park. We hadn't been to Phoenix before and we didn't know what to expect from a Phoenix crowd. One of the subtle things you pick up from traveling the country is the difference in the fans from region to region. In the sixties, the fans down South tended to be rowdier than the fans in the Northeast. The girls in the Midwest did a lot more screaming, and California was a mixed bag depending on what city and venue you played. We would often make little changes in our show depending on where we were playing and the size of the crowd. Sometimes we even dressed differently depending on what part of the country we were in. Part of the reason was that the crowds we were drawing had a lot of kids but also a lot of people over thirty. Things are more homogenized now, but back then, the country still hadn't made up its mind about rock and roll.

When we arrived in Phoenix, it was the middle of the afternoon, a beautiful sunny day. The only thing we were really told about the show was that the crowd would be huge and that it would likely be a very young audience, everything that rock and roll is supposed to be: summer, a lot of high school kids, and school's out. Our limo was met at one of the entrances of a perimeter that was so far away from the stage you could hardly see it. We had to leave the limo and get into a Brinks armored truck. As we started to move through the crowd we could hear and feel banging on the side of the truck. It took about twenty minutes to get backstage. I didn't know if we were the first act, the middle act, or what. Everything was very disjointed. The promoters slapped us on the back and within minutes we were on stage in this incredible band shell. Our instruments were already there. The band plugged in their guitars and we opened with "In the Midnight Hour." The roar of the crowd was awesome. There were thousands of kids moving back and forth and forward and backward. The whole crowd was in motion and the sound was intense, louder than we were.

We followed up with "Say I Am" and "It's Only Love." While we were playing, I was trying to make sense of the crowd. I couldn't tell whether they were standing on the ground or on seats. The whole crowd was moving as one. There were people who had climbed up trees and lightposts. As we started "I Think We're Alone Now," the crowd suddenly began to surge forward. It happened so fast it was like a tidal wave. The security was pushed back toward the stage, the concrete barricades were pushed over, and there was a gigantic crush of people against the stage and the screaming I could hear was different from anything I had ever heard before. You could see it in the faces of the kids right up front who were getting crushed. And the crowd wouldn't or couldn't stop surging. There was nowhere else to go except onto the stage.

We made it through one verse of "I Think We're Alone Now" and began to look for help from security, the police, the promoter, anybody. It was like being attacked. Suddenly someone stopped the show and we were hustled offstage so fast we didn't have time to think, except that we knew people were following us onstage from the crowd. We ran into the armored car and someone slammed the door closed. As we started to move out, the banging against the Brinks car was so furious that we kept moving from side to side to try to keep the crowd from tipping it over. When we finally reached the perimeter again, we jumped back into the limo and took off down the street. We felt like we were on the lam. When we got back to the hotel we went up to our rooms and started laughing. We had been through some crazy gigs but nothing like this one. A few hours later we were told that two girls had died that afternoon during our set. They had been crushed to death by the crowd. Dozens more were injured. There was nothing anyone could say or do, but we kept the faces of those girls in our minds for months, at first so happy, and then so terrified and confused, just before we were pulled off the stage.

While we were out on the summer tour, I was constantly coming back to New York to work on what would be the *Gettin' Together* album. While I was away, Bo and Ritchie did the final mix for the single, which I wasn't crazy about, but it got great airplay and became our seventh gold record. But things had definitely changed. Ronnie wanted to get married, so I called Diane up on the phone and told her I wanted a divorce. Diane didn't put up a fight. My son was about two years old. It was one of the worst things I ever did. I was thinking only of myself. I married Ronnie in Miami and met her family, including her uncle Red Pollack, who ran the Newport Hotel. The Newport was connected with the Jewish Mob and Santo Trafficante. I didn't quite put together who all these characters were until later, but it was overwhelming. I was like a Mob magnet. If I'd known everything, I might have been more concerned about my relationship with Ronnie than I was, but her immediate family had nothing to do with the Mob. Red was a nice man who treated me well and asked me if I would play at his hotel, which we did many times. The Newport was a gorgeous, swinging place right on the ocean, and a lot of big names came through there. Red was a very fancy, sharp businessman who worked with some of the same people who helped set Morris up in business before he established himself in New York. It was here where he likely first met Morris Gurlak. Gurlak had been Morris Levy's partner from the beginning. He was a soft-spoken gentleman who had a fatherly demeanor, and Morris Levy was very deferential to him, very sweet. Together, they created M & M concessions, which originally handled hatcheck and darkroom business. Back then, all the nightclubs would take pictures of the guests, and by the end of the night they would have them printed fast and fitted into a flimsy cardboard frame for sale, as a memento of your wonderful night at Birdland or the Embers or the Hot Spot, or wherever. That was where Morris got his start. Eventually they wound up owning not only the concessions but the nightclubs themselves.

Ronnie's father worked for the post office and would send returned samples from the drug companies up to Ronnie; samples of everything—antibiotics, pimple medication, whatever came through. Massive amounts of pharmaceuticals were sent through the mails back then to doctors all over the country, and Ronnie's dad would put together a kind of care package of undeliverable samples and send it up to New York. It was all very innocent. He thought he was helping by saving the kids (us) some money. We always had samples of the latest cold remedies and headache and flu medications. One of the packages had Dexedrine and Dexamyl and probably Eskatrol in it. I asked

Ronnie one day what they were, and she said, "Oh, they're diet pills, they help you lose weight. They also make you stay up forever." So I took one and went to the studio and I felt beautiful. End of story. I loved it. And I had a cornucopia of choices sent to me every month by my innocent and well-meaning father-in-law, who thought he was doing me and his little girl a favor.

When we got back to New York, we moved into a bigger apartment in the same building, 888 Eighth Avenue. Ronnie redecorated the whole place and started educating me in many ways. She gave me a more sophisticated sense of myself. But as sophisticated and cool as I thought I was, there was always a nagging sense of guilt about what I had done to Diane and Brian. I sent money home all the time. I would go there when I could. When I was going out west or coming back from the West I would try to stop by. I would bring Brian expensive but ludicrous gifts for a child his age, like a reel-to-reel tape recorder. They were silly things that I used to try to make up for all the time I was not spending with him. He would come up to New York a couple of times a year and I would go back just as irregularly. These were crucial years that I should have spent with him and I didn't. I was too busy becoming Tommy James.

The first week of August 1968, Morris was already bugging me about getting the next single in the can. One afternoon, I went over to Bo's apartment unexpectedly and caught him getting high as usual. He answered the door, invited me in, and immediately started talking about Morris. "He's fuckin' me, Tommy. Every time I ask him for my royalties I get some lame excuse. Morris is never going to pay me." While he was on his tirade, I saw a demo lying on top of his piano. I went over to look at it and it said, "Get Out Now—Bobby Bloom— Regent Sound Studios." I asked Bo what this was and he said, "Just something I'm working on." "Can I hear it?" I said. He got really uptight and said again, "It's just a thing I'm working on." "Well, let's hear it." So he played it, and it was a great little record, commercial as hell, and whoever Bobby Bloom was, he had a killer voice. I knew I had walked back into my "Gettin' Together" nightmare and caught Bo giving another of the songs that should have been mine to somebody else. I said, "You know, Morris is busting my ass to get the next single done." "Fuck Morris." I said, "Can I do this song?" He said, "I don't know." I asked him where he came off giving another artist his best stuff, when I was the one who made him a hit writer. He said, "Fuck, now I got to deal with you too, right?" I said, "You don't have to deal with me at all." But I knew Bo had a point, and I understood his predicament and even sympathized with him. The real point was that none of this would have been happening in the first place if Morris would have played straight. But I was not going to let that jeopardize my career.

I walked out and went right over to Roulette to see Morris. "Well, it's happened again," I said. "Bo's done a great record with somebody that should have been ours. It's called 'Get Out Now' and I want to do it." At which point Morris called Bo and said, "Get the fuck up here." I knew how that was going to play out so I left. I also knew that things were going to come to a head between me and Bo.

While Bo and Ritchie were putting the track together for "Get Out Now," I had to go out on the road and do a couple of dates. When I got back about a week later, Ritchie asked me if we could go into the studio the following night to do the vocals. I said sure, and the next night I headed for Allegro.

When I walked in, I saw the control booth filled with people. I said, "Ritchie, what's going on?" He said, "Bo brought a bunch of his friends down." I said, "I don't want all these people here while I'm doing a vocal." Ritchie calmed me down and I tried to make the best of it. They were some of Bo's musician friends and their girlfriends. Bruce and Ritchie both knew I was really upset. A recording session is a very intimate thing. There are always mistakes, flubs, missed notes, and many retakes before the record is just the way you want it, but we went ahead anyway. I listened to the basic track that Bo had put together with the musicians during the week and I went over the lyrics with Ritchie.

Even though it was tense in the room, I started out on the first verse. Before I was through, Bo hit the talkback button and said, "No, no, you're singing too hard. Sing the verses a little softer." At that point I was starting to get angry. Bo was obviously showing off for his friends and the whole damn thing was becoming so disrespectful I could hardly keep from yelling. We started again, but about twenty seconds into the vocal, Bo hit the talkback button again and hollered, "I can't believe how fuckin' stupid you are." There was silence for a second and then he said, "I said it's got to be softer, softer." I looked at him and I couldn't even move for a second, I was so enraged. I felt myself getting ready to explode. I slowly took off the headset, put it on the music stand, and walked into the control room.

Bo had on a Nehru shirt with a high collar and beads. I grabbed the neck of his shirt with my left hand, tore off his fuckin' love beads with my right—they went bouncing all over the floor—bent him over his chair, got in his face, and told him, "You open your fuckin' mouth to me again, you mangy little cocksucker, and I'm going to split your fuckin' face open right in front of your fuckin' friends."

He just gurgled a little. He didn't say a word. When I let him go, he fell off his chair and hit the floor and didn't move. I grabbed my briefcase and jacket and walked out. Needless to say, the session was over. I walked home feeling really bad and I knew that was the end with me and Bo. There was no way that we would ever work together again.

A couple of weeks later, Ritchie and I went into the studio and finished the record. It charted for us, but it was the most joyless hit I ever had.

By now the IRS had literally set up shop at Roulette. Morris was so contemptuous of them that he actually gave them their own office down the hall from Normand Kurtz. We were all on a first-name basis. They came virtually every day, dealing mostly with Howard Fisher, who would always politely provide them with some set of books, which they would dutifully examine on their fishing expedition. Their confusion and dismay was always intensified when one of "the boys," Morris's non-music-business-related associates, came up for a chat.

Billboard magazine had its year-end awards and I was voted Male Artist of the Year. I was honestly surprised because the Shondells and I were never considered heavy or hard rock, but also because Morris had a real hatred for *Billboard,* and I couldn't blame him. The three big trade papers were *Record World, Cashbox,* and *Billboard. Billboard* was always the most difficult to deal with. *Cashbox* had a slant toward retail. It focused on the money generated from records. *Record World* had a slant toward radio airplay. *Billboard* claimed to be in the middle. The problem with that was that when you put out a record, things back then happened fast.

In six weeks, you needed a new record, that's how quickly the turnover was if you wanted to stay constantly on the charts. If you put out a record and it generated some excitement, it immediately went on the radio. That would be reflected in *Record World.* But it would take two or three weeks after you heard a song on the radio before the sales figures would start to hit and the stores would report it. That was when your record would start charting in *Cashbox*. So there was a lag time between those two trade papers. *Billboard* claimed to chart records in between radio play and sales. But you would always be two to three weeks further ahead in radio airplay than you were in sales. You might start out in the Top 20 in airplay. Then if the record was a hit it would usually climb very fast, which meant you might be number one in *Record World* but only number twenty in *Cashbox*. *Billboard* took the average of the two, and listed you as number ten in their paper. That sounded okay, and you might eventually go to number one in *Cashbox* and *Record World,* but you would have to stay that way for three weeks to get a number one in *Billboard*. There was always a controversy about *Billboard*'s top five lists, because the whole industry was screaming at them over the discrepancies and nobody as loudly and as rudely as Morris. He was always on the phone with the editor. "We went number one in both trade papers and you got us at number six, fuck you and your charts." That was a phone call that happened often. And now, because the other trade papers collapsed over the years, *Billboard,* by attrition, became the keeper of the flame. When young researchers and historians go back to check the archives for a record's history, they inevitably get a skewed sense of how popular it really was.

Christmas of that year, Morris threw a huge party at the Roundtable, which was his club. The Roundtable was a big place with a three-tiered layout that gave it a sunken aspect, as if you were watching a show at a theater. The top tiers were a kind of semicircle with tables looking down on the main floor, where the stage was. You walked in on the upper level and walked down to ringside. The booths were big and round and the stage itself was a huge O. Morris had reserved the whole club for this party, and Ronnie and I had the best seats at Morris's table, just to the right of the stage. It had a lavish Moroccan décor to go with the belly dancers and the food. Morris Gurlak was there greeting everyone and by mid-afternoon everybody from Roulette was settling in. Howard Fisher and Red Schwartz were there. Normand Kurtz, the in-house lawyer; Nate McCalla, his bodyguard and partner at Calla Records; and Jerry Schiffron. George Goldner was there; all the wives and girlfriends were there; and Morris was in great spirits. It had been a sensational year for Roulette, and Morris made every effort to impress. He seemed to have taken great care in presenting a kind of show for us. When the belly dancers came out, he would laugh and say, "Watch this . . . watch what she does here." And the girl would twirl something on her left breast and Morris would be pleased. The food and booze were incredible and never stopped coming. People from the record industry stopped by. This was a celebration of pride in what Roulette had accomplished and Morris wanted the entire industry to see. I felt great because I was at the center of it. The Shondells and I were now the premiere act in the Roulette stable. All the other pop acts, all the other Latin and jazz acts now paled in comparison. In fact, Tito Puente and Joe Cuba, both Roulette acts on Morris's Latin label, Tico, were on stage performing for us. Joe Cuba did a hit he had called "Bang Bang" and another called "Push Push Push." J. J. Jackson stopped by and did his smash "But It's All Right." J.J. was signed to Calla Records and was Nate McCalla's biggest success. Then the Shondells and I got up to perform. We did an abbreviated set, playing all of our gold records up to then. As a special surprise, we did a song I used to do back in Niles with the Tornadoes. I would often take two songs that I liked that had the same kind of feel and glue them together to make a tight little medley. One of my favorites was "Little Latin Lupe Lu" and "Killer Joe." I had this in mind because Morris loved Latin music. I figured we were never going to record the thing because Morris didn't own the publishing, but I wanted to do it as a kind of Christmas present for Morris. We started to play and Joe Cuba's band picked up on it right away. All of a sudden I had a six-piece horn section cranking out notes like a chorus. Tito Puente joined in on his steel drums. People got out of their seats and started dancing around the tables in a conga line. When we finished, we got a standing ovation.

Even beyond the fame and adulation, the screaming crowds and the gold records, this party was the fulfillment of everything I had ever wanted. This was my world, and if I wasn't the king, I was sitting next to the king. I was at the king's table.

At some point that night, Morris and Nate took me into the men's room and Nate pulled out a vial of crystal meth. I was dumbfounded because up until that time and even afterward, I never knew Morris to use drugs at all except perhaps an occasional joint. Drugs at Roulette were strictly forbidden, especially considering Morris's associates and the Treasury boys always snooping around. Nate pulled out a silver spoon and he and Morris stuffed their noses with this stuff like they were born to it. They offered me some but I did not join in because I was already doing enough pills to blow the top of my head off and I had been washing them down with booze. They had what looked like a pound of the stuff and they were flying. It was very uncharacteristic of Morris but this was his empire and he was judge, jury, and law. When we got back to the tables everyone was hugging and kissing everyone else. I knew Nate was high because he became very emotional as Ronnie and I got ready to leave. He grabbed both of us in headlocks, one under each arm, squeezed us, and kept saying over and over, "You guys are the best." "God bless you." Nate would normally never be that effusive in a million years.

I was absorbed in the success and the glamour and celebrity of it all. But it was more than just being a star. I had found a new family and it was Roulette. I was like a lion cub in the den. I might get growled at and slapped occasionally, and I could feed only when the leader of the pride let me, but I was safe and secure. I had a new wife, I was artist of the year, and everything was beautiful. And these were all my new best friends whose sole mission was to promote me, sell me, help my career, and look out for me. I felt warm and protected. There were Morris and Nate. There was Red, whom I loved. There was Howard, who never wrote the royalty checks I was supposed to receive, and Karen, who never signed those checks, and Morris, who never authorized them. But I didn't care. This was my family. And here were all the other members of the family. Here was Tommy Eboli, alias Tommy Ryan, who was the head of his own family and loved my music. Here was Dominick Cirillo, alias Quiet Dom, who always kept Karen company when "the boys" were in discussion in Morris's office. Here was Vinnie Gigante, alias "The Chin." And there was Tommy Vastola, alias Sonny Vastola, alias Corky Vastola, alias Gaetano Vastola, alias whatever. Everybody proud and happy. Everybody glad to see me. Everybody looking out for me and watching me.

Oh, I had a new family, all right . . . Oh brother, did I ever.

CHAPTER SIX

Mony Mony

After the incredible year we had in '67, by almost every standard we were an astonishing success. In fewer than two years we had nine hit singles, five smash albums including our first *Greatest Hits* album, plus *Billboard*'s coveted Artist of the Year award. We were playing dream gigs all over the country to packed arenas and baseball stadiums, and we had a constant barrage of radio airplay. But as usual, being Roulette artists meant not being paid, and it was becoming a tormenting issue. It wasn't just me, everybody connected with the Shondells was trapped in Morris's demented financial black hole. And yet, in a way, the whole Roulette payment debacle started to become my responsibility. Everyone would come to me because they were too afraid to confront Morris. I was becoming the shop steward for most of our team—the band, photographers, publicity people, art designers, sometimes even the studio. The joke about "the quietest place on the planet" being accounts payable at Roulette was no longer very funny. I would get reasonable pleas from our crew for payment that I would pass on to Morris. "Yeah, yeah, I'll get to it." But nothing would happen and the demands would eventually grow into fury and frustration because Morris would parade around Roulette as if nothing was wrong. What made matters worse was that Red and Karen were always clueing me in about Morris's stately living; his luxury Manhattan penthouse, his condominium in Florida, his mansion in New Jersey where he lived with his fourth wife, Nome, plus a newly acquired dairy farm in Ghent, New York. Then there was Morris's endless supply of special girlfriends and his passion for gambling and prostitutes. He had plenty of money for all that but never a dime for all the people who made it happen, especially me.

It wasn't that I was living in poverty. We were making great money from radio airplay and concerts. Lately we were doing commercials for product lines like Real Girl Cosmetics and HIS clothes. We also had an arrangement with Philco doing "hip-pocket records," miniature 45s about as big as a modern-day CD, which needed a special player, also made by Philco. But there were always lean periods and those were the times I had to ask Morris for an advance. I never made an appointment for these encounters so I could catch him off guard. But I seldom fooled him for long. He knew what I was there for.

I can still see him puffing on his Pall Malls, no smile, waiting for me to make my move. It was almost like we were stalking each other. He would grunt, "How ya doin'?" and I would start out very cheery, tell him some news about what record we planned to put out next. Usually I had a tape of the next single and then I would pounce. "Morris, can I get an advance?" But Morris could play this game better than anybody and any threat to his power was immediately squashed. There were times when he would say in his gruffest voice, "Not now. See me next week." And you had to slink away. If he was feeling generous he would yell for Karen or Howard Fisher and have a check cut. "The kid needs ten grand," like he was doing you a favor. But it was not a business negotiation, it was psychological warfare. Mor-

ris had to first make you understand that he knew he owed you
the money, and that you were not going to get it if he didn't
feel like giving it. With me, he knew when to throw a bone, but
there was never any doubt who was in control, and he made me
aware of this a hundred times, that I was not going to be treated
like a respected artist, like a human being. A few thousand here,
a few thousand there; that was the closet I ever got to royalties.

If I got the advance, I'd usually walk out feeling grateful for
having money in my pocket . . . until I realized how much the son
of a bitch really owed me. In the beginning I actually fell for the
line he would always spew about studio costs. "You're spendin'
a fuckin' fortune in the studio." "You're putting me in the fuckin'
poorhouse." Right, you don't sell twenty million albums and singles in eighteen months and still lose money for the record company, especially when Morris got all the publishing rights.

The walks home after my confrontations with Morris were a
shrink's dream. I would run the scene over and over in my mind
and become more and more enraged. How I would have to go
into his inner sanctum and fall on my knees and then have to
listen to his bullshit, and how he would take an almost demonic
glee in making me sweat and beg. His method was to use all the
power of his office, his Mob connections, his reputation for bru-
tality, but even more than that, his pathological need for money,
especially other people's money. Power and money were what
his psyche, his soul, was made of. His peculiar dementia was that
he had to make you understand at a visceral level that he was
prepared to blow everything to hell, destroy the very thing that
was making him his millions, unless you submitted to his will.

And how could I stop him? How could anyone stop or control him? All the lawyers I hired were either bought off or scared
off. Everything in my life and my career was tied up in this guy.
And it was slowly taking its effect on the Shondells and Ron-

nie because it was slowly taking an effect on me. I was becoming a stranger to myself. I didn't realize the extent of it at the time, but Morris was infecting me somehow. His rages were slowly becoming my rages. It didn't happen overnight, it was more insidious than that. It crept up inside me and I was helping feed that beast with all the drugs and booze. At first, popping pills was fun, it was part of the scene, part of the creative process. It kept me awake so I could finish a recording session or a show. But now it was getting uglier. I was becoming dark, and making people afraid of me, which in a twisted way I felt I had the right to do because it was being done to me. I felt tortured and trapped. I had never dealt with someone that I needed so much from on the one hand and at the same time was like a schoolyard bully I couldn't get away from. I also knew that somehow, somewhere, sometime there was going to be a confrontation. I knew that Morris and I were eventually going to go head to head and all this rancor was going to spill out. In a sense, a strange but unmistakable part of his sick theater was that Morris was almost daring me to do just that. There was no other way Morris could have a relationship with anybody except the guys who were even more psychopathic than him. The guys who hung out at Roulette. The guys who were his partners and protectors.

In February 1968, Bo had his own confrontation with Morris. Even after everything that had happened between us, I felt sorry for Bo because I knew how things would end up. Simply put, he hadn't been paid a dime since he started at Roulette. Morris owed both him and Ritchie a fortune in royalties as producers and writers going back to "I Think We're Alone Now." In his own twisted logic, Morris took the attitude that if it wasn't for him, Bo wouldn't have anything. "I gave you Tommy James. I can take Tommy James away." The way Morris treated Bo crystallized his psychotic need for control and his pleasure in vengeance. He'd rather jeopardize all the future hits that Bo might have produced for me and him than pay Bo the tiniest portion of what he legitimately owed him. He told Bo that if he left, he, Morris, would make sure he'd never have another hit. "I'll fucking see to that." And he never did.

So Bo went over to Laurie Records and Kazenetz and Katz. He got some kind of position over there as a producer. He still couldn't take writing credits because the publishing still belonged to Artie Ripp and Kama Sutra. So Ritchie went too. He felt that he owed Bo that and maybe he could straddle the fence between me and Kazenetz and Katz. In the meantime, Morris went a little crazy trying to find me a producer. I talked with Wes Farrell, who was already a legend, and Joe Wissert, who was producing the Turtles, plus some others, but there was really nobody I wanted. I felt I was ready to start producing my own records, and I had something specific in mind.

Early in 1968, I went into Century Sound Studios, which was Brooks Arthur's studio, and started putting a track together. I liked Century Sound because it had a lot of history. It was where most of the Phil Spector stuff was recorded. My home base studio, Allegro, was closed for one of its periodic upgrades. I wanted to make a party rock song, a throwback almost to the great Gary U.S. Bonds and Mitch Ryder records I loved so much. A throwback like "California Sun," which drove me crazy back in Niles so long ago and was written by that great songwriting team Henry Glover and Morris Levy. This was the beginning of what would eventually become "Mony Mony," although at the time, we had no name for the thing. We did not even have much of a song.

It began life as a simple rhythm track: with Pete Lucia on drums, a friend of his named John Andiolorro on bass, and me on guitar. We had more of an idea than we had a song, and that is where it began: a beat; a groove; just three or four chords and we were going to write the song around the track. I knew I was going to slice and splice it later on, but that first night, for our purposes, I liked what we had.

After about three weeks, Allegro Studios finally reopened, and by this time, Ritchie Cordell had come back. He didn't like it with Kasenetz and Katz. He had a problem with Jeff and Jerry. "They don't fucking get it. They're a couple of slave drivers." Bo was still over there but Ritchie had had enough. Ritchie was too much of a free spirit to be corralled in the semicorporate world of prefabricated bubblegum on demand. I was glad to have him back.

We took the track I had on tape from Century Sound and went to work in earnest. We sort of did sound surgery on the thing, rewriting it technically. The song was literally sliced, diced, and glued back together. We had it in a hundred pieces and then put it back together the way we wanted it. In the reassembling, we created an actual melody with a verse and hook. By this time, we had been adding snippets of guitar, organ, piano, and lots of background noise. On any night, we would add a harmonica part, two hollers, and three screams. I think everyone I knew in New York was on this record doing something. We finally reached a point where we had glued enough track together to write the song.

The night before we were supposed to finish the record, Ritchie and I went up to my apartment, popped two Desbutals each, and started writing the lyrics.

"Here she come now sayin'—blah blah—blah blah."
"Wake me, shake me—blah blah—blah blah."
"Shoot 'em down, turn around—blah blah—blah blah."

We had all the nonsensical one-liners you could ever want but we still could not come up with a damn title. We knew we needed a two-syllable girl's name but every real name sounded stupid. We had to make up a rock and roll name like Sloopy or Bony Maronie. By about midnight, Ritchie and I were spent and we took a break. We threw down our guitars and went out on the terrace. We lit up our cigarettes, leaned on the railing, and looked out at the Manhattan night sky. All of a sudden, my eyes fell on a building across the street, a couple of blocks down. It was the Mutual of New York Insurance Company building. There was a neon sign on top of it with the logo on it: MONY. It had a dollar sign in the middle of the O, and the time and the weather underneath. And it kept flashing MONY MONY MONY. I slapped Ritchie on the arm and said, "Look." We started laughing. I said, "Is that God winking at you, or what?" Ritchie just said, "Unbelievable." There was our name. And it was a good thing too. We were under so much pressure to come up with something, if I had been looking in the other direction we would have called the song the Taft Hotel.

In the end, out of deference to Ritchie, I didn't take credit for coproducing the record. As far as the writing credits went, I put Ritchie's name on it because he helped with the words. Of course, whenever you put Ritchie's name on something it meant you were putting Bo's name on as well. Then Bobby Bloom came in.

Back in the sixties, everyone was a talent scout, and Bo and Ritchie had discovered this kid Bobby Bloom, who eventually had hits like "Montego Bay." He was very talented, and Bo and Ritchie wanted to produce him, so he was always hanging around. He came to some of my sessions and soon he was doing little things. He ended up doing the "OOO I love ya, Mony Mo Mo Mony" part. So I put his name on the credits too. Within a week, I was already working on what I wanted to be the follow-up to "Mony Mony," which as it turned out became the next hit single, called "Do Something to Me."

When I went up to deliver "Mony" to Roulette, we were all excited about it. The first person I played it for was Morris. "Is that the next single?" He liked it but he wasn't thrilled with it. He felt that it was too much of a throwback to the early sixties. It didn't sound like Tommy James. He wanted to put out a record that sounded more like "I Think We're Alone Now" because it had done so well. He wanted to put out a song called "One Two Three And I Fell," which was the last record Bo Gentry had been involved with. But Kasenetz and Katz were busy bastardizing the "I Think We're Alone Now" sound with acts like the 1910 Fruitgum Company and Ohio Express. In a kind of reverse logic, the critics were calling "I Think We're Alone Now" the precursor to bubblegum. I didn't want any part of it. Morris saw things differently.

Morris thought and reacted to music like the common man. He couldn't tell you how to make a hit but he knew one when he heard it, and that's not as elementary as it sounds. His gift was being able to market the stuff. Nobody was better at marketing rock and roll than Morris Levy. He was a natural-born salesman and he instinctively knew what would make money. He was very singles oriented. He was not an intellectual. He was also a bully, so whatever he couldn't do in a businesslike way, he would grab you by the collar and threaten you. That's how he closed the deal. He knew what he wanted and he wanted to make money. Morris played this role as a gangster and he was very convincing. Morris was also very good at knowing what he wasn't particularly good at. If you had a better idea than he did, he would say, "Run with it." His ego was not about creativity. It could have been records, it could have been lightbulbs.

To him it was just another commodity. And I think because he approached music that way, he understood the business better than anybody in the industry. This was one of those times. "Okay," said Morris. "Go with it."

Morris was not one to show up at the studio. But every once in a while he would be with someone he wanted to impress and he would stop by. I would show him a good time, order some Cokes and pizza. The night we were doing "Mony Mony," I had the studio filled with people. Not Morris's people, my own people. I had every secretary at 1560 Broadway down in the basement screaming on the record. I left word with Beverly, the receptionist, "I don't care who comes here, nobody gets in." So Morris picked that night to bring some of his friends in. He told the receptionist, "You tell Tommy, Morris Levy's here." Beverly said, "I'm sorry but I have orders. Nobody gets into a Tommy James session." Beverly was about four feet ten inches with a beehive hairdo and had a voice like a Queens debutante and a perfectly high-pitched nasal whine that could drive you nuts if you weren't in the mood. This was in front of Morris's friends. He finally got Beverly to call me. "There's a guy out here named Morris somebody and . . ." I said, "Oh my God, put him on the phone." I started groveling immediately. He had been humiliated in front of his friends.

My life at that time was in high gear. I became friends with Terry Knight from Terry Knight and the Pack, which later became Grand Funk Railroad. Terry used to be the lead singer but stepped down to become their producer and manager. Terry Knight's manager was Ed McMahon, who lived at Tower 53, a new building that had gone up on Fifty-third Street between Sixth and Seventh. Terry took me up to meet Ed and we spent a good part of the afternoon with him. I mentioned that I was going to be out in L.A. to do the Hollywood Bowl. He said we should meet up. Ed McMahon was sort of courting the youth vote at that time. I told him I would be staying at the Century Plaza and we would meet up after the show.

That afternoon before the Hollywood Bowl, I met Mike Curb, who was my age, twenty-one, but was president of the MGM film studio. It was a few weeks before *2001: A Space Odyssey* was released. He later became lieutenant governor of California under Jerry Brown. The Cowsills, who were managed by my agent, Lenny Stogel, were on the MGM label so we all got the cook's tour of the studio by Curb himself, who was very cool. He was very reserved and conservative and for a year or so had been quietly buying up MGM stock until he had amassed 51 percent of it. When Polygram/Deutsche Grammophon wanted to acquire MGM, much to the surprise of everyone, including the stockholders, Curb had the majority share and made a fortune in the buyout. I was very impressed. I was impressed by anyone who was actually being paid for their work.

After we performed at the Hollywood Bowl with the Rascals, I went back to the Century Plaza, where we were staying, and because I was still flying from my pills, I called Capitol Records and booked time at one of their recording studios. I had taken a tape of "Do Something to Me" with me to L.A. and finished a rough mix of the song that night. I don't know where I found the nerve, but I charged the entire session to Mike Curb. When I got back late to my hotel, the front desk clerk was all atwitter. Ed McMahon had dropped by my hotel with Frank Sinatra, and I'd missed him because I was so high I forgot about our date. I never could get with him again to make my apologies. I can just hear Sinatra mumbling, "Fucking kids," while he cooled his heels in the lobby waiting for Tommy James, who had stiffed him.

Morris was in high gear too. He had found a very lucrative niche in the cutout business. He had helped create two of the giants of that side industry of the record business, K-tel and Adam VIII. They would take records that were recent hits and put them out on compilation albums called cutouts. The problem was that Morris would go a step further and put hits that were currently on the charts out on the compilations, which was ridiculous from the artist's point of view because it devalued the existing record, already a hit single, by about 90 percent. It became worth a dime instead of a dollar. The reason Morris would do this to his own product was because, down to his very core, his essence, he was a pirate. He could not not be a pirate, even if it wound up hurting him, and me. He had businesses with Tommy Ryan and his childhood friend Sonny Vastola where counterfeits were manufactured and stored. A bootlegger, in the record business, is like somebody printing money. Bootlegging not only devalues your product, but it also floods the market with more product so each unit becomes worth less and less. If a record store is not buying your product from a reputable distributor, somebody else is making the money under the table, tax-free. Small businesses were forced to take Morris's counterfeits or else they would likely have their stores burned down. Of course, if Morris found out that you were bootlegging his product, he had a way of taking care of that. Usually with baseball bats and Nate McCalla. After 1967, nobody bootlegged Morris's records except Morris.

In 1968, Roulette moved from 1631 Broadway to 17 West Sixtieth Street, next to Atlantic Records and right by Columbus Circle. Roulette was expanding but it did not change the personality of the company. Every time the possibility arose of Morris going corporate, he nixed it; he would have been accountable. Many major labels including CBS and RCA wanted to distribute Roulette. Morris would never permit it. He would have had to honestly account to artists and pay them.

The office move triggered many audits. I don't know why. It might have been unintentional or coincidental, but it did. It got the government's attention. For the next two years, there was a even bigger stream of auditors, accountants, and IRS agents. To Morris, this was like a bug in his ear. "Get with Howard," he would snarl, and off they would go to examine still another set of books. Of course, no one ever talked out of school. It was the Roulette family's little secret.

It was a closed group of people. Roulette ran very efficiently because it had a dictator. Dictatorships always run smoothly. Whenever a major distributor wanted to talk to Morris, his standard line was "I don't have partners." When Normand Kurtz, the in-house lawyer, put together a nice overseas distribution deal, he expected to be included in the arrangement. "Fuck you, I don't have partners." Of course, Morris did have partners, lots of them. His partner for life was Morris Gurlak, the father figure who started him in business and continued in the hatcheck and darkroom concessions, in the restaurants and clubs that they owned together. He was a partner with Tommy Eboli in the cutout business. He was a partner with Alan Freed when Freed came to town and expected to take over the New York radio and concert business. He was a partner with George Goldner.

In some ways, having a guy like Morris in control was a great safety net. It was wonderful because nobody messed with you. You didn't make much money, but nobody messed with you. I had the run of Roulette and anything Roulette was involved in. And Morris trusted me with big budgets, my own career, and business decisions involving master recordings of other artists that he was thinking of buying in order to secure the publishing. "Is this a hit?" And Morris fascinated me as no other person had before. Sometimes I would sit with him for hours talking and asking him questions about the music business, politics, philosophy. I even talked to him about Jesus or something that had a spiritual connotation to it and that would always get a good laugh, "That's great, that's a good one," like I had just told him a joke.

Morris was the kind of guy who would trust you once and if it worked, he might trust you again. But the Roulette Regulars were different. They were the big boys and their business was big business. And everybody had his role. Howard received the monies, Nate collected what was owed, and the flow of Genovese crime capos in and out of the office was astonishing, each with his own private deal controlled or financed by Morris. Morris had his own private back exit accessible through a secret door in his office, in case he ever needed a quick escape.

One reason I knew I was unique in Morris's world was because he never really signed another rock act. There were occasional new acts like the Three Degrees, but most of it was fluff. If I was with a Columbia or an RCA, I could have easily had a couple of hits and then got lost in the shuffle. At Roulette, I was the golden boy. Whatever I wanted, except my money, I got. In Morris's world, the artist was always in debt against the studio and recording costs, and no matter how many records you sold, you never seemed to make a dent in that. I could not even get the gold records I had been awarded. I used to get drunk or high and steal them off the wall. Morris would come into Roulette and see the gaps on the walls and yell, "Where the fuck are my gold records?" The secretaries would say, "I thought I saw Tommy James walking out with them." "That fuckin' kid."

In 1968, I had a falling out with Lenny Stogel, my manager. I just didn't like the way things were going. He had a secretary that I really liked named Joanne Adler, and frankly I wanted to start my own management company and I knew I could with Joanne. Morris gave me an office for a production and management company. When Lenny was out of town, I got all my books, records, and photos, and told Morris to inform Lenny he was out, which he did, and I never heard another word from Lenny. If I had done it myself he would have sued the hell out of me.

"The kid's with me now." That was that.

Joanne let everyone know that I had my own management company and that was where you were to call if you wanted Tommy James. The phone rang off the hook. We got more calls then Roulette did, and that was saying something. Interviews, concert dates, and publicity appearances. The only person I had to answer to was Morris, my fairy godfather, and he let me do anything I wanted to do.

It felt like a family but it functioned well on a business level. I was still on pills but back then diet pills were not considered dope. It was what was prescribed by your doctor when you needed a boost. It was medicine, it was diets. One of the residual effects was that you didn't sleep for four months, but so what? I got the job done. My entire universe had become reduced to about ten square blocks. My apartment, the studio, Roulette. Red had made me the darling of radio. He constantly worked the phones. "Tommy's coming out with a new album, a new record, and a new sound." Whatever it took. And radio was playing my album cuts as well as my singles.

I tried to get back to see my family and I managed to do so about four times a year, but it was lame. Brian would be sent up to visit me in New York City, but it was so unnatural. The life I was living was great for a twenty-one-year-old who was in the record business but it was no kind of world for a child. I would be buried in the studio all night, doing interviews and organizing logistics for my gigs, and I would bring my three-year-old son into this lunacy. I had become a Christian but I really wasn't living my faith. Of course, spirituality back then often meant another toke on your pipe. I was living in Tommy's theme park rather than living a normal life.

The only person who ever tried to put brakes on me was Morris. Morris had been aware for some time that the band and I were popping uppers. The night Frankie Lymon died, Morris made one of his rare trips into the studio. Morris and George Goldner had signed Frankie and the Teenagers years ago, and they had the monster hit "Why Do Fools Fall in Love." Frankie had stayed with Roulette but had become a drug addict. Morris watched as Frankie's career declined and his life fell apart.

One night, in the studio, Morris took one look at the ashtray on the console filled with crushed diet pills that I was getting ready to snort and took me off into a corner. That's when he told me that Frankie had died of a drug overdose. "This is what's going to happen to you if you don't stop taking those fucking pills. Every time I talked to this kid he was high." He meant Frankie. "Knock it the fuck off." And then, as an afterthought, "You know, if you die, the price of your catalog is going to go through the roof." It was still another side of Morris. He cared and he was looking out for his property.

I didn't need Frankie Lymon to get me thinking about drugs. I had something much closer to home. That summer, I got word that Craig Villeneuve, my original keyboard player, had overdosed and died.

CHAPTER SEVEN

Crimson and Clover

At the same time as "Mony Mony" was out and climbing the charts, March 1968, Bobby Kennedy declared his candidacy for president. I was actually very happy about that because I had always been a big Kennedy fan and it was always my view that the sixties were all about trying to get that Kennedy feeling back again after it was crushed in 1963. To me, it was more about that than about rebellion against the war and all the suspicion that began to infect America. It seemed like no matter what rock you lifted there were maggots underneath. When Bobby finally announced, it was tremendous. Lyndon Johnson virtually conceded defeat by refusing to run for reelection.

Everybody I knew seemed to feel that way but we never thought we would actually become involved in the political process. "Mony Mony" was huge in America but it was even bigger in Britain. "Mony" was one of the biggest records Britain ever experienced. Morris had put together a string of foreign deals, most of them in Europe, with an outfit called Major/Minor. Normand Kurtz handled the arrangements.

In early May, we got a call from the Democratic National Committee in Washington asking us if we would be interested in getting involved in a political rally. Roulette took the call and passed it on to Lenny Stogel, who was still with me at the time: "The Democrats want you to do a campaign rally in Union Square Park." Union Square was at Seventeenth and Broadway at the beginning of lower Manhattan, and a popular spot for rallies and protests. Robert Kennedy and Eugene McCarthy were scheduled to speak. We were shocked but rather proud that either party would think we could motivate a political campaign. We were not what you would call outspoken, but we accepted without hesitation. If they wanted us, we were happy to get involved.

On the day of the rally, which was midweek, we took three limousines and drove to the park. Lenny and his entire staff went with us and lots of people from Roulette, including Red Schwartz. It was a beautiful spring day and all the flowers in the park were in bloom and the breeze was balmy and sweet. There were thousands of people crammed into the park, standing on benches, sitting on tree limbs, huddled around the statues, and a few thousand more had spilled out into the surrounding streets, which had been blocked off. There was a makeshift stage and in front of it were lots of very longhaired protesters who had taken over that space. They carried signs that were mostly anti-Johnson and anti-Humphrey. Humphrey was seen as the establishment candidate early on and was attached to Johnson at the hip. For better or for worse, he refused to directly repudiate Johnson's foreign policy, which was not making him many friends. After all, it was the Democrats who had made a mess of the war, and all the goodwill that Lyndon Johnson had after JFK was murdered had evaporated long ago. When we took the stage, these belligerent kids up front, carrying signs that read DUMP THE HUMP, started yelling at us: "Sellout! Sellout!" We were kind of upset by that but there was so much anger registered against Democrats, that anybody supporting the party in any way was considered a sellout.

Mayor Lindsay, Bella Abzug, and other local politicians were making speeches. We arrived in the afternoon. The newspaper press and television reporters were everywhere and at one point the police even threatened to charge the protesters. There were a lot of strong, silent guys with dark glasses talking into their cuff links. It got a little scary once or twice. But we played, and everybody seemed to settle down, listen to the speeches, and generally enjoy themselves. We had a recording session later that night, so we did not stay to hear the real stars.

Afterward, we were thanked by representatives from the Democratic Party. They said we had done a great show and asked if we would be interested in appearing at any more rallies. We said sure. That was enough to put us on a short list of entertainers who were willing to get involved in the presidential race. No one called for a couple of weeks and we forgot about it. But eventually someone did call and asked if we would appear at the upcoming California primary, which was to be held the first week of June. Would we consider playing at the Ambassador Hotel? We wanted to very much but we had already committed to playing the World Teen Fair in Dallas on June 3. We regretfully declined because the dates were just too close together.

The World Teen Fair was held at a gigantic complex like McCormick Place in Chicago and there were many acts playing simultaneously on different stages throughout the week. There were at least two dozen big-name acts that were all having hits at the time, like the Mamas and Papas and the Buckinghams, plus a lot of up-and-comers. During our stay in Dallas, I became friendly with a female reporter who worked for the *Dallas Star*, and wound up spending the night at her place. The next morning, she promised to take me to the airport, but since we had some time to kill, I begged her to drive me through Dealey Plaza and she did. A few months before, on a plane trip, I had sat next to one of Jim Garrison's secretaries and found that he was reinvestigating the Kennedy assassination. She told me they had discovered Kennedy was shot from four, maybe five different directions, and I had to see this for myself.

I was mesmerized, standing in the middle of this placid little corner of Dallas at the exact spot where JFK was killed. I could not believe how tiny the place was, as opposed to the expansiveness you sense from seeing it on television. There was the book depository, the grassy knoll and the fence, the bridge by the overpass, all the possible angles of opportunity, even the storm drain that might have been a factor. I stayed there until the cops finally came and chased us away, which apparently happened often. How could I not help thinking of Bobby and that we had been asked to play out there tonight?

But I caught my plane and flew home, returning to the apartment near midnight, and I turned on the television to see how the voting was going. I wanted to see which act had taken our place when Frank McGee's voice broke into the commentary and said, "Hold it, hold, it . . . there's apparently been a shooting at Kennedy headquarters." I was horrified and too tired and strung out from a weekend of rock and roll and pills to feel anything but despair. I stayed up with Ronnie, transfixed by the television and what proved to be a deathwatch. In my delirium, it felt like I had been through two assassinations in twenty-four hours, not to mention that Martin Luther King had been gunned down a month before. I think it was Gore Vidal who was asked a little later on what hero Americans could turn to and he said, "None, this country shoots all its heroes."

The whole country was up for two days and eventually Robert Kennedy died. That ended the sixties for me. The magic and the good feelings shriveled up and died with Bobby. I went into a depression because I felt so close to the events and the man. I am sure it was partly fueled by pills and booze, which I did non-stop for weeks after the killing. It was a terrible loss of belief in everything.

Then two things happened that pulled me out of my funk. "Mony Mony" just exploded in Britain. It was the biggest record they had ever had in the sixties as far as singles sales. It had been number one for weeks, so the BBC called Roulette to ask if we would do a tour of Britain culminating with a nation-wide appearance on their *Bandstand*-type show called *Top of the Pops*. We agreed. It would get us out of the country, into a new world of adulation and success. Why not? They started a nationwide publicity blitz anticipating our arrival.

But then we got another call right after we agreed to the tour. It was from Hubert Humphrey's office. Humphrey's assistant, Ursula Culver, asked if we would appear with the vice president on his campaign trail. We would start traveling with him after the nomination. I felt it was our duty to do whatever we could to keep Nixon out of the White House. We were honored. It was the first time a rock act had hooked up with a presidential cam-paign in any real way. I tried to explain this to the BBC. They would have none of it. They banned our records. They were very upset and didn't play any of our records for almost five years. I hated to lose Britain, but tough.

We were supposed to meet Humphrey in Wheeling, West Vir-ginia, after the convention. Ritchie Cordell, Mike Vale, and I were up at my place in New York writing and high on pills. We had the convention on. Suddenly all of Chicago exploded. Kids were getting their heads beaten in. The cops were mounting an armed attack. It went on for hours. Mike and I said, "What have we got ourselves into? Is every rally going to be like this?" It seemed the whole country was exploding. Humphrey was nominated the following night at about 2:00 A.M. It was an understatement to say his campaign got off to a bad start.

We met him the following Wednesday. We flew down on a prop plane on which the wings were above the cabin and you could see gasoline running down the windows. We landed and then were driven in golf carts to another hanger at the airport where Humphrey was going to speak. We went inside and they had a makeshift stage set up with American flags all over the place. We changed and went up on stage and were introduced without any sound check. The Secret Service were everywhere and they were on high alert. We played about five songs. They put folding chairs up on the stage, and we sat by Mrs. Humphrey in our stage clothes while a contingent of local politicians made speeches. One guy actually called the vice president "Herbert" Humphrey. Flashbulbs were exploding, and Humphrey came up to great applause and made an impassioned speech. TV cameras caught the event and the campaign was off and running.

We transferred to another puddle jumper, a Convair, for the next campaign stop. On the plane, Humphrey finally came back to meet us. "Well, Tommy James, how are you?" I got up and hit my head on the overhead bin. "OOO, are you okay, young man?" He spoke in that high-pitched chant he always had. "Thanks for joining the campaign." We went on to two more campaign stops, in North Carolina and Georgia.

Mr. Humphrey wanted us anytime we could make it. They gave us our own Learjet from Butler Aviation out of LaGuardia Airport. Our itinerary was taken care of. And so we joined the campaign. We must have done more than fifty big rallies in all. In the meantime, we were performing our own dates, but we and the campaign coordinated everything.

We played at Binghamton, New York, at a coliseum. There were flyers and posters up all over town: "Appearing One Night

Only: Tommy James and the Shondells," and then underneath, in small letters, "Also appearing Vice President Hubert Humphrey." We got top billing. Humphrey would walk out on stage after our set and say, "Look at these crowds, Mr. Nixon," and, of course, they credited us for the crowds. Our rallies had metamorphosed from airport hanger to coliseums of 20,000 to 30,000 people.

There were many other celebrities that appeared as well, but we were the only ones who appeared all the time. In Yonkers, we played a rally and had to pick up Shelley Winters at her Upper East Side brownstone. We took a couple of limos. She climbed in, and after she said hello, she hit the bar and downed a quick pint of scotch. Of course, we were all high on pills. Alan King, the comedian, was master of ceremonies and met the limo. Shelley got out with her glass of booze and we all went to the stage. We played our abbreviated set first and then took our place on the dais with Mrs. Humphrey on one side and Alan King on the other. Alan was thrilled and was without his trademark air of disgust that got him so many laughs. "This is going to be great," he said. Finally, Shelley Winters took the podium and almost fell over. She was slurring her words. "I'm an actress and I can say any damn thing I want, and I say Hubert Humphrey is going to be the next president of the United States." At least she got his name right. Alan King turned to me and said, "Every time this fucking broad shows up, we lose ten thousand votes." What Alan did not know was that the stage was miked to pick up the applause when the politicians spoke. His critique of Shelley Winters went out through the sound system and the whole auditorium heard him and started to roar. He just put his hand to his forehead and sank into the chair.

Once during the campaign Humphrey called me up and asked if I would come over to his suite. I was with Pete Lucia and the two of us went up to see the vice president. His doctor was there and a bunch of party officials, and Humphrey was holding court in a corner of the room. We were taken over to the couch where he was expounding on something. After he finished, he floored me by asking if I would consider heading a president's council on youth affairs. It would be a kind of sub-cabinet position because he wanted to stay in touch with young people. I said something stupid like, "Mr. Vice President, the youth of this country are definitely having affairs, and I'm just the guy to look into it." If you hang around politicians enough you start talking like them. We laughed and then I said I'd be honored. Then he asked us for our opinion on something he and his advisers had been working on. He then proceeded to tell us his plan for ending the Vietnam War. "We want to have a national referendum as soon as I get in office. We want to end this thing. It'll do two things: it'll show the world what democracy really is and also save about thirty thousand kids." I couldn't believe we were hearing that, because the news media was just chomping at the bit to hear something like that, but he refused to espouse it publicly because it would have been a slap in the face of Johnson, and Humphrey felt Johnson was responsible for his being the nominee in the first place. Johnson, by the way, had yet to endorse him. We knew we were hearing history but we were sworn to secrecy.

We often went up to his suite to talk about the issues of the day, his latest speech, and how the day's rally had gone. Some nights were more animated than others. It was almost like after a gig with everybody sitting around, winding down. One night he said, "I'm exhausted and I've got to stay up and write this darn speech." And I said, "You know when I have to stay up I sometimes take these stay-awake pills." And I took out a vial of black beauties and gave him one. Looking back on it, I can't believe I did that, but that shows you the times. The next night he said, "Geez, those things are powerful, I was up the whole night." "Well, if you need any more," I said, "just let me know." He never asked for them again. His doctor must have given him the heads-up.

We were there the night of the election at the Leamington Hotel in Minneapolis. I can't begin to tell you how electric that scene was. It was so exciting because of how much was riding on this election, the assassinations months before, the convention, the war—we felt like we were at the center of things. And we were. The hotel was filled with celebrities like Gene Barry, Lee Majors. All the TV networks were there. We were actually on all three at once and we played a couple of sets waiting for the results to come in. Nixon had begun months before with an outrageous lead in the polls, somewhere around 30 percent. By election night, the candidates were neck and neck. Humphrey credited us with the bump in the polls, and though I don't think we played that crucial a part, we were tickled with the compliment.

The whole night was a party. Mike, Pete, Joanne, and I went up to Humphrey's suite and Lee Majors came over. He was drunk as a skunk, tried to hit on Joanne, and wound up spilling his drink down her blouse. I said, "That's it," and pushed him away. He said, "Fuck you," and pushed me back, and we had to be separated. I almost got into a fistfight with the Six Million Dollar Man on the night of the presidential election. By the end of the night, I was just as bad as or worse than Lee Majors and there was still no winner announced.

Suddenly the buzz at election headquarters was that the voting machines in Chicago had broken down. Nobody knew what was going on in Cook County. Later that morning, a flood of votes went Nixon's way and he was projected the winner. Everyone knew what had happened. It was Mayor Daley's revenge on the Democrats for his national humiliation at the convention.

What a letdown. It really looked for a while like Humphrey was going to win. The next morning can only be described as a national hangover. We had breakfast with Mr. and Mrs. Humphrey, and everyone wanted a recount because we were all convinced the election was stolen. He refused. "Mr. Nixon is our president now." Then he paused a moment and said, "This guy has a terrible habit of getting himself in trouble. You have to watch him. He didn't get the name Tricky Dick for nothing. He's going to need all the help we can give him, because he'll find some way to screw it up."

It was just one of many disappointments in 1968. The success of "Mony" was offset by the BBC ban. We all had so much hope for and faith in Robert Kennedy, and then he was shot. Then Hubert Humphrey was really trying to change things, and he was beaten in one of the shadiest election coups ever. To go through everything and to end up with Nixon, after all that. No Camelot II, no Humphrey, more and more Vietnam with no end in sight.

Before the 1968 election, there was very little left-right, conservative-liberal dichotomy. That election, that year, was when we lost our unity and became a red and blue country. Divided we fall. There was a real sense of trauma at the end of that election and Humphrey was correct. We did lose thousands more kids.

Humphrey and I stayed friends. In 1975, I did a concert for UNESCO. We did a show at an arena in Hanover, Maryland, and I was presented with a plaque from the State Department. Hubert Humphrey gave me the award. We stayed in touch up until the day he died.

When you're out on a campaign it is very much like being on

tour. There is a lot of downtime. As we traveled on our Lear-jet we had a lot of opportunity to check out the competition. What we discovered amazed us. Everybody was buying albums. It was like going from reading poetry to reading novels. Eight-track tapes came out on the market with accompanying boom boxes to play them on. Before that point, you could hear an entire album only on your stereo at home. Albums didn't travel well. You never heard an album outside of your own rig. Now they were portable. Pete Lucia had an eight track and he would bring the latest albums out and we listened to them religiously: the hot new bands were Led Zeppelin, Blood Sweat & Tears, Crosby Stills & Nash, Joe Cocker, Neil Young. All album acts.

When we left for the fall campaign, it was a singles market and we were part of it. When we got back, it was an album market. All of our friends had fallen by the wayside. It wasn't the Rascals or the Association anymore. It was King Crimson, Led Zeppelin: the album acts. We knew that if we wanted to survive in this business, we would have to become an album act. We could not stay pop any longer. That's when we began the *Crimson and Clover* album.

We went into the studio toward the end of the campaign and produced the "Crimson and Clover" single. I am convinced that that single allowed us to make the transition to the next level of our career. No other project before or since would have allowed that to happen. The single was finished in December, having taken us about five hours. I don't think we ever moved so fast in the studio. I played most of the instruments, Mike played bass, and Pete played drums. It was gearing up to be the most important release for us, because in order for it to be successful it would have to be the major turning point for Tommy James and the Shondells. Roulette put its entire promotional and sales appa-ratus in high gear. That night, I finished "Crimson" and made a rough mix, right off the board. We were going to come back in a week to mix in a lot of ambient sound, a lot of echo. We wanted it to be a more profound statement than was on the mix.

But I was so excited I stopped by Morris's office. "Is that the next single?" Morris listened and gave me his blessing. He thought the record was going to be a monster. For days after I played him the record he kept calling me up at my apartment. "This is a fucking number one record." He also told me, "I'm very proud of what you did with Humphrey. You know he was a liberal before it was fashionable to be a liberal." Morris never talked to me like that. I did not know he knew words that big. He wanted to know everything we did on the campaign. "How the fuck did you pull this off?" I had impressed Morris Levy. At the office the next day, I ran into Nate McCalla, and he was just as giddy. "We're all proud of what you're doing. Keep up the good work." Morris and Roulette had been following our Humphrey tour with pride. I found out that Morris had told everyone he knew, including Tommy Ryan and the boys. Considering the fact that we destroyed sales in Britain, which meant a pinch in Morris's pocketbook, he should have been furious, but he wasn't. Morris never said anything about the lost revenue. He treated me like I had graduated from Harvard.

That weekend, the Shondells and I played a date in Chicago and we were met at the airport by a limousine. As we were driving to our hotel, I stopped by WLS on the off chance that program director John Rook was there. I wanted to get some reaction to "Crimson" from a radio station that had always been so good to us. John was in that afternoon and invited me to sit with him. He made a big deal out of me being there. I did an interview and talked about the new single. I should not have done it, but I played him the rough mix when we were off the air. He flipped over the record. "Let me get Larry Lujack in here. We just hired him." Lujack would go on to be one of WLS's top DJs. Rook played Lujack the rough mix and without my knowledge or approval pushed a record button on the tape recorder and made himself a copy. Lujack loved it. They handed me back the tape and we parted with promises to call each other next week. By the time I had gotten into the limo, the radio was tuned to WLS and Larry Lujak was announcing in his best DJ voice: "World exclusive . . . Tommy James and the Shondells . . . brand new single . . . 'Crimson and Clover.'" He was playing the rough mix on the radio as a world exclusive. I knew I was never going to hear the end of this from Jim Stagg. I was warned on "Mony" not to give WLS an exclusive.

Monday morning, when I stopped by at Roulette, a five-foot funeral wreath was sitting outside Red Schwartz's office with a banner that read: "Condolences on the death of Tommy James and the Shondells at WCLF Radio." It was from Jim Stagg at the rival station. Morris came right out and said, "What the fuck?" I told them both what had happened. Red called Rook and told him about the wreath. Jim Stagg wouldn't take Red's call. Rook said, "Fuck Jim Stagg, I'll play it every twenty minutes." And then he added in radio lingo, "He'll have to go on the record." And that is what he did. This was still the rough mix. I never got a chance to remix the record.

Morris had DJ copies sent to all the radio stations in the United States. He wouldn't let me do a final mix. So the single of "Crimson and Clover" that we all know was from the tape of a rough mix that was never supposed to see the light of day.

"Crimson and Clover" took off and was the biggest record we ever had. Jim Stagg left WCLF not too long afterward. As it turned out, it was more his funeral than mine. The record broke all over the world, except, of course, in Britain.

CHAPTER EIGHT

Crystal Blue Persuasion

We had been asked, by FM radio, to make a long version of "Crimson and Clover" for the album. They thought it would be a cool thing to do and I agreed. The Shondells and I went into the studio, and because of the history of the record, we had to make a long version out of the short version. It is usually done the other way around. I had to take pieces of the track and stitch them together to make a six-minute version from a three-minute version. When I mastered the original single, I ever so slightly sped it up. We did this occasionally because the slightly faster speed worked better on AM radio. The variable-frequency oscillator had just made its way into the studio. It was a device that allowed you to speed up a tape without doing anything mechanically different to the tape recorder by using the current that was coming through the wall. Normal current came through at 60 cycles. If you raised it to 61 cycles, it meant that you were putting a little more power into the tape recorder motor and everything would speed up relative to the amount of current. If you went to 62 cycles it would speed up more, if you went to 59 cycles, it would slow down. This was a revolutionary way of altering tape speed without fooling around with the mechanism.

When we mastered "Crimson and Clover" at Bell Sound Studio, we did not use the oscillator because Dom, an engineer at Bell, was expert at an esoteric art form known as "wrapping the capstan." He would take a little piece of Scotch tape and wrap it around the capstan of the tape recorder. Doing that sped things up as well. The problem with that method was that it was never exactly 61 or 62 cycles. It was always 61.3 or something like that. Our final mix was now slightly faster by this one loop of tape. We had to speed up the master to the exact speed the single was running at. We had to go back and forth and back and forth. We finally got it right and made tape copies of the first two verses without the background vocals because we had to put guitar solos on for this longer version. We used steel guitars and fuzz guitars and it came out nicely except that when we glued it all together, there was a difference in tape speed we could not account for. None of us knew this, but it took the oscillator about ten minutes to completely warm up. And we had created the tape copies before it had a chance to completely warm up. It was just a breath slower than it was supposed to be. The only way I could synchronize it perfectly was if I went back to the drawing board and started the entire process over again. So we said the hell with it, no one will ever notice, and we glued the new tape we made into the old master tape. So for thirty years, every time the long version came on the radio I always heard the drop in tone and it drove me crazy. When Rhino Records bought the masters from Roulette in the late eighties, Bill Inglot, the engineer, finally fixed it digitally. Just a normal day in the studio. Is it any wonder we were always high on pills?

We also started work on "Crystal Blue Persuasion." I had played a gig awhile back in Atlanta and a young fan had come over to me with a poem he had written. It was a Christian poem inspired by the book of Revelation and contained the phrase "crystal blue persuasion." I never heard from this kid again. I was so taken with the poem and particularly that phrase that I knew I wanted to use it somehow in a song. Eddie Gray came up with the opening riff and it was exactly what I wanted, airy and ethereal with a Latin feel.

"Crystal Blue" was the hardest record we ever made. When we first recorded the song it was filled with instrumentation, heavy guitars, drums, and very complicated arrangements. It tended to be lush and overwrought, and when we heard the playback, we didn't like it. The track did not match the song. So we went back into the studio and began taking things out, which was exactly the opposite of what we normally did. We produced the record and then unproduced it. We kept extracting practically everything we had put in, and the more we took out the better it sounded. By the time we were finished, there was little more than a flamenco guitar, tambourine, a very effervescent bass line, and a conga drum. But it was a hit and I knew it. I could feel it in my bones. I did not release it right away as I normally would have, because the "Crimson and Clover" single was still selling and receiving endless airplay. And by now we were ready for the release of the album.

The *Crimson* album was released just before Christmas 1968. Vice President Hubert Humphrey wrote the liner notes. It was the hottest record in the country and we were booked to do our first *Ed Sullivan Show* the following February. At the time, it was the biggest show on television and for years had been the high-water mark of success in the industry. It was the most watched show in the country, every Sunday night. Because "Crimson" was screaming up the charts, we were the hottest group at that moment. The *Crimson* project made us keenly aware that if we did not score with this album we were finished. We had gotten rid of all our production crew, and the Shondells and I created *Crimson* as a self-contained unit. We wrote the songs, played the instruments, produced and arranged all the material, and even designed the album cover. As much as I loved being left alone by Roulette, it meant that all the responsibility was on us. I felt I had to show Morris something. If we had failed with *Crimson*, I don't think we could have picked up the pieces. Appearing on *The Ed Sullivan Show* was our vindication and laurel wreath. Otherwise, it would have been like the funeral wreath that Jim Stagg had so graciously sent me months before.

Several weeks before our appearance, we had done several dates with the Beach Boys, who had done the Sullivan show many times. The week before we were to go on, we stopped by their rooms at the Hyatt House in Los Angeles. They were going to walk me through all the protocols because preparations for an Ed Sullivan appearance took all week. No matter what your status in the entertainment world, it was a scary thing appearing with Ed. The Sullivan show could break as well as make careers. The Beach Boys and I were watching that Sunday and I was particularly interested because Ed always came out at the close of the show to announce who the headliner would be for the following week. Sure enough, just before the end of the show, Ed stepped in front of the camera and said, "And next week on our show, for all the youngsters . . . Tony Jones and the Spondells." We looked at one another. "Great. He never heard of us and he can't read." It got worse.

Tuesday morning we went to the Sullivan Theater because you had to commit to being on the set, around the clock, for several days. They wanted us to do the show live and I begged them to let me do a lip sync. They always insisted on live performances but they would compromise as long as I could give them a four-track tape with different layers of sounds so they could regulate the output and not have it sound like the record.

I went to Allegro Studio, which was just across the street. I mixed a four track of "Crimson," but instead of giving them different mixes, I gave them different levels and different EQs, which meant they couldn't fool around with the mix, but the needles on their machines would be jumping around. All they could do was change the volume. They never caught on and I got to do a lip sync, which took a lot of pressure off because there was no way these guys were going to get the fade at the end of the recording of "Crimson and Clover." That was a train wreck waiting to happen.

Each day they marched us progressively into the final show. It was literally a zoo backstage because there were always hundreds of people, animal acts, the Vienna Boys Choir, a guy practicing his spinning plates routine. Our show included John Byner, Stiller and Meara, and Sergio Franchi. They custom built a stage set just for us. The band was on platforms at different levels and they shot us against funhouse mirrors that would slightly distort our features: an Ed Sullivan acid trip. As we were watching the dress rehearsal on Sunday, Bob Precht, who was both the producer and Ed's son-in-law, walked over to me with that week's copy of *Billboard* opened to the chart page. He tossed it on my lap. "Crimson" had gone number one at that moment.

In reality, *The Ed Sullivan Show* was almost live. They taped a show before a live audience from 5:00 to 6:00 and then took an hour for dinner. Then they taped another show before another live audience from 7:00 to 8:00. At 8:00 P.M. sharp, they went on the air and the production crew ran both tapes simultaneously and aired the best performance. They were incredibly skillful at split-second timing.

At the end of the show, if you were the headliner, you got to talk to Ed. It was another thing the Beach Boys had warned me about. While the acts were performing, Ed would stand in a narrow alcove watching the show on a little black-and-white TV set. He would also unwind with a little nip. We finished our last song and Ed, who by this time was on his sixth scotch, called me over. "Now, Tommy, I understand you were born and raised in New York City." I froze. Where the hell did he get that info? I could not let that stand because I had relatives and friends watching and the whole town of Niles was glued to their sets. "Well, actually, Ed, I've lived in New York City for a couple of years but I was born in Dayton, Ohio, and raised in Niles, Michigan, but I've lived here since I was eighteen." I gave him every opportunity to exit gracefully. He wanted none of it. "Once again born and raised in New York . . . Tommy James." At least he got my name right.

After the show we all went down to the Copacabana to celebrate. Jackie Leonard was the headliner. I walked in with Ronnie, who was dressed in a gothic-style gown. My hair was hanging down my back. The maitre d' sat us ringside. It was too good for Leonard to pass up. "Oh, it's a male witch and Lady Gwendolyn."

If that wasn't enough to start the year off right, I received a letter from my draft board announcing my change in status. When I divorced Diane and married Ronnie I lost my 3-A classification. Married with child was good enough for a deferment. I was still married and still had a child but the State Department did not see it that way. I was reclassified 1-A and the week following *The Ed Sullivan Show* I was due to appear at my local draft board for a physical. I was upset and the only person I could talk to about this was Morris. I told him I had a problem. Morris didn't say anything except to tell me not to worry.

I tried to get my psychiatrist to write a letter saying I was a bed wetter. After hearing Hubert Humphrey's dread prediction about the Vietnam War, I was really in a funk. I worked in the studio the night before my physical and stayed up popping pills all night long so I would look my best in the morning. Nate McCalla picked me up at my apartment at nine o'clock and drove me to my appointment. It was horrible, but I felt better with Nate with me. He was a decorated veteran of the Korean War and was as relaxed as could be. The first thing that happened when I walked in was that I was recognized. When you are on *The Ed Sullivan Show,* everybody remembers. I spent the first couple of hours signing autographs and shaking hands. It was sort of like getting a physical in an airport terminal: "Ah, Tommy, before you bend over and spread your cheeks, could you sign this for my wife?" I went through the physical and psychiatric exams but I must have looked like a zombie. I wasn't pretending to be crazy, I was just being myself and at this time in my life, that was one step away from being a bone fide mental case. I answered all the questions from the psychiatrists and went out to the waiting room to hear the sentence.

When the whole ordeal was over, you had to walk up to a three-man tribunal and get your draft card. When they handed it to me I could not believe it. I had been classified 4-F. Nobody was getting 4-F in 1969. It just did not happen. I looked at the sergeant who handed me the card and said, "What's this?" He did not say a word. He looked at me and pointed his finger at the side of his head as if to say, "You're nuts." Nate grabbed me and said, "Let's go." When we were outside, he had a sheepish grin and said, "I told you not to worry." I found out later that as soon as I left Morris's office after telling him about the draft board he went to work. One of his friends on the board of directors of Chemical Bank was also on the Selective Service Commission.

* * *

On February 14, 1969, Valentine's Day, Vito Genovese died of a heart attack in the federal penitentiary in Atlanta, Georgia. This caused a major earthquake at Roulette. Morris's partner Tommy Eboli had been the acting boss of the family ever since Vito was sent to prison, which meant he was the liaison between Vito and the rest of the family, giving Vito's orders to the boys, making sure they were followed, and keeping Vito up to date about business. It always amazed me that this went on for nearly eleven years, right under the noses of the guards, but that's the way it was done.

For about a week after Vito's death, Roulette almost stopped being a record company. Business wasn't getting done. Morris was in and out of the office and nobody could talk to him. Guys I had never met before, and didn't want to meet, suddenly descended on the building, going into Morris's office and then leaving as if on a mission. Nate McCalla pulled me aside one afternoon and told me, "Don't walk in or out of the building with me."

I would always watch Red carefully at times like this. He always seemed to know what was going on, especially when things got weird. I took my cues from him. He came to work as little as possible, and the few times he showed up, he barricaded himself in his office with the door shut. When I finally got in to see him, he had his head buried in his hands. He had just talked to Karen. "Nobody fuckin' knows what's going to happen, if there's going to be a power play, or what. Anything could happen with these fuckin' guys." I thought to myself, *How fucked up is this?* I come up to talk about *Crimson and Clover,* and I get this shit. I felt totally helpless and I wasn't even sure if I should hang around. I stayed home for a few days, and Ronnie and I followed the story on TV. They talked about it on almost every newscast. They even talked about who the new boss would be, like it was some sick soap opera. They flashed pictures of the top candidates for the job, including Tommy Eboli.

About a week later, I went up to Roulette. Red's door was still shut but things seemed to have calmed down a little. I went into Red's office and he said, "Sit down. We have visitors." "What do you mean?" "The boys are in Morris's office. All of them." "You're shittin' me?"

We talked about seeing the whole story on the news. Red was trying to act normal, calling radio stations. All of a sudden, Karen rang Red. "Is Tommy with you? Morris wants to see him."

"Oh shit!" I slowly got out of my chair and stood up. Red just looked at me and shrugged his shoulders. I turned around and walked out of Red's office, kind of weak in the knees. "Why the hell does Morris want to see me?" Morris was standing in the doorway of his office waiting for me. I looked for some kind of clue from him as to what this was all about but there was no expression on his face. He just said, "Hi, I want you to meet somebody," and came around and put his hands on my shoulders, and walked me into the office.

Inside Morris's office, it was eerily quiet. Sitting on the L-shaped sofa and some scattered chairs were half a dozen very serious-looking men, with very solemn faces. Morris shut the door, which he never did, and walked me over to a guy sitting on a chair. He was leaning forward, elbow on knee, with his right hand cupping his chin. He had a shock of black hair and wore a white dress shirt opened at the neck and black slacks. "This is Mr. Gigante." I knew this was serious shit. Morris never called anybody "mister." Mr. Gigante shook my hand and said, "Hey." This was Vinnie "the Chin" from the Genovese family. I had just seen him the other night on the news as one of Vito's possible successors. Morris turned me toward the sofa and said, "This is Mr. Cirillo." Better known as "Quiet Dom" Cirillo. I used to see him talk with Karen once in a while when Morris was having meetings, but had seen him more recently on TV. Next was a heavy, bald-headed, scary-looking older guy with a cigar sticking out of his mouth. I knew who he was because I had seen him several times on TV. It was "Fat Tony" Salerno from the Jersey wing of the Genovese family. He would later be immortalized as HBO's Tony Soprano, just as Morris would be portrayed as the character Hesh in the same show. Morris hadn't said anything this time, so when I went to shake Fat Tony's hand, Mr. Cirillo said, "This is Mr. Holiday." Maybe they were afraid I'd recognize the name.

Next came Mr. Vastola, whom I knew already as Sonny Vastola, another member of the Jersey clan. Then Morris said, "And you know Mr. Eboli." Everyone but Sonny would eventually become heads of the family over the next four decades.

With his hands still on my shoulders, Morris said to all of them, "He's a good kid. He's got the number one record this week." They all gave a collective, deep-throated grunt of approval. "It was nice to meet you all," I mumbled. Morris said, "We'll talk later," and I left the room.

As I was walking back to Red's office, all I could think of was how many murders, crimes, and God knows what else I had just shaken hands with. But I kept wondering, what was this all about? Was Morris showing me off? Was he letting me know who he was? Was I in some kind of danger because I could place these guys in Morris's office? My head was spinning. A few days later, I learned that Roulette Regular Tommy Eboli, alias Tommy Ryan, was elevated to capo di tutti capi, the boss of bosses. Morris's buddy and business partner was now officially the head of the Genovese crime family.

After the big meeting, Roulette was really humming along. Morris actually seemed happy. It seemed like his troubles with the IRS had vanished. One day, they packed up and left and I never saw them again. "Crimson and Clover" was on the charts for a long time but we decided to do something different. We released "Sweet Cherry Wine" as a follow-up. This was an aberration because "Sweet Cherry Wine" was not on the *Crimson and Clover* album. We recorded "Sweet Cherry" after we recorded "Crystal Blue Persuasion." I wrote "Sweet Cherry Wine" with Ritchie Grasso, who was married to Morris's secretary, Karen, so politically it was a good thing.

Morris loved "Crystal Blue Persuasion." He was crazy about it because it had a Latin feel. Morris, half Spanish, loved Latin music. Tito Puente, who I had become friendly with, also loved "Crystal Blue" and did it in his act. Roulette was always a big promoter of Latin jazz. I was riding high on pills and during this string of hits I went through one of my periodic rages over money. It was around this time that my contract was running out. It was common knowledge in the industry that Morris and I were going to have to renegotiate. I thought this might be a good time to pressure Morris. But Morris and I never discussed the issue man to man. It was always handled by my lawyer, Howard Beldock, and Morris's lawyers. Other people had their eye on my contract. Clive Davis let it be known that he was interested in acquiring me for Columbia Records. Everybody was playing coy.

My marriage at this time was showing signs of cracking. We weren't having a terrible time, but I was taking pills every day and then drinking to come down off the pills. Ritchie Cordell and I were getting high a lot. We often went up to Bath, New Hampshire, with Ritchie and his wife because Ritchie liked to get away and shoot guns. He had a fascination with firearms and I caught the bug as well. I wound up buying a lot of guns. I bought a .22 pistol, a .25 automatic pistol, a Browning .22 magnum machine gun, a Marlin .22 with an octagon barrel, and a .32-caliber police pistol from 1902. It had a rubber handle and an eight-inch barrel. I brought all the guns home with me, which was a big risk because it was clearly against the law. I didn't care about that. I stockpiled ammunition and occasionally I was shooting target practice off the deck of my terrace, trying to take out lightbulbs or hit the water tower across the street to make it leak. Ronnie was not very happy about that. My obsession reached a peak when I started carrying a pistol every time I went to the studio. I convinced myself that I might be in danger from every derelict walking home at 4:00 A.M. I was also worried I might be in trouble from my association with Morris and Roulette. People may have been looking at me as an "associate" of Morris, the way Morris was an "associate" of Vinnie the Chin. I was also seeing a psychiatrist.

At that time, seeing a psychiatrist was kind of trendy, but I really needed one because I was becoming a lunatic and the guns were getting troubling. My shrink was Dr. Sumner Goldstein, and every Thursday I would visit his office in a beautiful brownstone. One afternoon at Dr. Goldstein's office, as I was pulling a pack of cigarettes out of my briefcase, one of the pistols I always carried fell out on the floor. There is very little in the way of covering that kind of thing up. The doctor looked at me and said, "What the hell is that?" "Oh, that? That's my gun." I took the bullets out and showed him. He took it, hefted it, and gave it back. I reloaded it and put it back in my briefcase. He said, "You carry that thing around with you?" "Yeah, you never know." One of our main topics of conversation was Morris's refusal to pay me. He also knew how I felt working for the Genovese crime family and their cadre of killers and hoodlums.

Dr. Goldstein put two and two together and came up with ten. He was convinced that I was going to shoot Morris.

My doctor did not waste any time. He called Morris. One afternoon I came home from the studio, and sitting in my living room was Ronnie; my secretary, Joanne; Morris; Morris's bodyguard; and Dr. Goldstein. I stood there, frozen. Morris said, "We're going to take the guns up to my place." I was having an intervention before there was a name for it. Morris said, "Follow me," and we walked into the bedroom and out onto the back terrace. He suddenly grabbed me by the collar and lifted me off the ground so my feet were dangling. I was so high that I started laughing. "What the fuck you doing?" I could not stop giggling. I could hear the New York traffic below and the wind blowing in my face while Morris, with his hand on my throat, pushed me against the wall. "Do you know what I did to the bum who killed my brother?" Morris's brother had been murdered at Birdland back in the late fifties. "I fucking took a knife and stuck it in his fucking stomach and twisted it"—he took his other hand and pushed it into my stomach—"I stuck it in his fucking stomach until his guts fell out." When Morris put his hand in my stomach it tickled, and now I was really giggling. "Really?" I said. Morris let me down and then started laughing himself. "No, you ain't going to hurt me, are you?" As we walked out of the bedroom he said, "Look, you come up to my place." Morris had a farmhouse in Ghent, New York. "You can shoot anytime you want. You don't want no guns in the city. It's no fucking good." Then he paused and said, "You scared walking home? I'll send somebody."

The next thing I know they were packing my arsenal up— by now I had more than a dozen guns—into suitcases, garment bags, and any boxes I had around the apartment. "With all the crazy shit I did in my life," Morris growled at me, "if I get pinched with this junk, you're going to hear from me." He and his driver, a young kid who was a black belt, took my weapons stash down the elevator and out to his car. I found out later that the kid was also Nate's bodyguard, so he must have been quite a terror. And what did that say for Nate? You know you've reached a certain level of infamy when a bodyguard needs a bodyguard. From that point on, a Sicilian gentleman named Dom stopped by my apartment every Wednesday or Thursday, whenever I went to the studio. I remember he was a big Mets fan, he was good at beating people up, and he was an amateur photographer. It was fun making small talk with Dom. Once he asked me where I was from and I said, "Michigan." He looked at me like he had never heard of the place. I said, "Michigan. You know, where they make all the cars. Like Studebakers. My uncle used to design Studebakers." "No kidding," said Dom. "My cousin Bobby used to steal 'em." He always carried a gun and a 35-millimeter camera. He hung out with me at the studio and took a lot of pictures. They were so good, we used them on our second *Greatest Hits* album. It was predictable of Morris's luck that he found a photographer he would not have to pay.

"Sweet Cherry Wine" was a monster hit record. Later in the summer we released "Crystal Blue Persuasion" and that exploded. It was played immediately and everywhere, except Britain. Those two plus "Crimson and Clover" were thought of as a threesome because they came so fast after one another. That year, we became the first group to outsell the Beatles in single record sales.

We went on to record what would become *Cellophane Symphony* at a new studio called Broadway Sound at Broadway and Fifty-fourth Street, above some street-level stores. It was beautiful and brand new. The men who owned the studio were there to meet me, and one of them was Whitey Ford from the

New York Yankees. He was half owner of the place. When I checked out the control booth I saw this monstrosity, a contraption that looked like one of the old switchboards from the 1920s. I asked what it was and they told me it was a Moog synthesizer. I asked what it did, and they said, "Listen to this." It mimicked every sound imaginable, woodwinds, brass, strings, and percussion. So we made an album around the synthesizer. We recorded blues, pop, jazz, and ran it through the "synth." We were the first act to actually use one of these things that has now become standard in any recording studio.

That day, I went out to lunch with Whitey Ford. There was nothing more ridiculous-sounding than me trying to talk baseball and Whitey trying to talk music. The conversation as I remember went something like this:

WHITEY: No, actually that was the Boston Red Sox, not the Boston Celtics. They're a basketball team.
TOMMY: No, actually Buddy Holly's group was the Crickets, not the Beatles. The Beatles are British.

Cellophane was not as popular as *Crimson* because of its experimental nature, but it got us a lot of airplay on FM radio. The Shondells were selling albums to the hard-core hippies, which was hard to do. For some reason, in the late seventies the album inexplicably took off out of Cleveland and got a second life.

In August we went to Hawaii to do a two-week combination gig and vacation. Everybody took their wives. "Crystal Blue" was number one, and we played in Hilo and Honolulu. We had a great reception but the big event was the volcano that was in the process of erupting. The place was overrun with volcanologists and geologists. We decided to take a look. We drove down at night, and there was a gate that was left open and a sign that read "Crater Rim Road." We did not know that we were not supposed to be there. We found ourselves on the rim of the volcano and the entire road was carved out by lava flow. Our throats were burning from the sulfur. If we had stayed any longer, we would have died from asphyxiation.

In between gigs, we stayed at a beautiful mansion at the foot of Diamond Head, on an old sugar plantation. The Rascals, who were on the gig with us, were staying down the street. The sea wall came right up to the back of the house. We had Polynesian servants waiting on us hand and foot. While I was relaxing with a mai tai on the veranda, I got a call from Roulette from my secretary, Joanne. Artie Kornfeld was the Cowsills' producer, and a very successful one out of New York. Artie and I were friends and we even had the same attorney, Howard Beldock. Beldock called Joanne and said Artie would like to know if Tommy could play this gig he was helping to promote. I said, "Where is it?" She said, "It's on a pig farm in upstate New York." I said, "Are you nuts? You're asking us to come back to New York, to leave paradise and fly halfway around the world to play a pig farm?" "Well, it looks like a pretty important gig, a lot of people are expected, and a lot of acts have already committed . . ." I said, "If we're not there, tell them to start without us." Just before the weekend the news about Woodstock was making all the TV news shows and we knew we might have made a mistake. There was nothing to do but go back to enjoying Hawaii, which I did. In fact, the next day I was floating in the sea just offshore when a huge tropical bee stung my water raft, almost drowning me. After the final gig we were taken back to the airport, and I boarded a plane with a bucket of fried chicken and a .22 automatic pistol that had eluded Morris's search and I had hidden in the bucket of chicken. No one ever knew.

The Atlanta Pop Festival was the next big rock concert and it was a very heady affair. Janis Joplin was there and we had a nice talk. She told me she loved me because I reminded her of Ricky Nelson, who was her favorite act. They brought us in by helicopter onto a makeshift helipad. It was at a race-track and there was no way to drive in. It was the only time in my life I ever rode on a copter. I was pretty high and the only other thing I remember was that the act just before us was Sha Na Na. Everything was gargantuan. It was incredible to see 600,000 people. We got sloshed in the dressing room on Southern Comfort and Jack Daniel's and the usual smorgasbord of pot and hash. From what I understand, it was better organized than Woodstock. All the bands liked it more and the crowd was better treated. It was another three-day festival. "Crimson and Clover" was such a great crowd pleaser but it was also incredible to be taken into the hearts of the other acts. "Crimson" was accepted by the fans who were focused on psychedelic and "heavy" music. They took it as part of our transformation from pop to more gritty rock, so we were able to play "Mony Mony" and "I Think We're Alone Now" and also be accepted by the hard-core fans. Everybody just had fun. Our expectations about "Crimson" were spot on. We were so lucky to have that record at that time.

The Atlanta show was actually part of a southern tour. A few days later, the mayor of Baton Rouge, Louisiana, gave us the key to the city. We were flying another propeller plane and the plane could not take off. The pilot had to recalibrate and try again. There was just too much weight. As soon as we made altitude, we flew smack into an electrical storm and got struck by lightning. I could see oil trickling down my window as we tried to navigate through the storm. The lightning actually does not hit the plane; it goes around it and creates a vacuum under the plane. It opens up the sky and the air underneath is split open. The bottom fell out of the sky and we dropped five thousand feet in a matter of seconds. I was sure we were going to crash. There were people screaming and crying but somehow we made it.

Pete Lucia and I flew out separately during this tour and went from Memphis to Atlanta, on another propeller plane. It was us and about a hundred service guys. There was visceral hatred. A few whistles over our hair, but it wasn't even good-natured anymore. We were all about the same age. The only reason I wasn't one of them was that Morris Levy had pulled me out of the fire.

We released three albums that year. *Crimson, Cellophane,* and *Greatest Hits Volume II.* Morris, who would never fly on an airplane, drove out to Las Vegas and invited all twenty-eight independent distributors along for a weekend of gambling and hedonism. These distributors were spread all over North America; distributors like Malverne, All State, Select-O-Hits, and Navarre. On Friday night they all had envelopes shoved under their hotel doors with a hundred-dollar chip in each and Morris's blessing to have a good time. They would talk on Sunday morning. He took care of the rooms and all the other expenses. On Sunday, with each distributor hung over and probably a little chagrined, Morris announced his firm's intentions. "The new Tommy James *Greatest Hits* is going to ship platinum." He put his finger on each man's chest and said, "You're taking two hundred thousand copies, and you and you and you, a hundred thousand each, you understand me?" They understood. Each one left sweating blood but no one resisted. They wouldn't have done this for anybody else in the industry.

Once the distributors took all the albums that Morris shoved down their throats, *Tommy James and the Shondells: Greatest Hits Volume II* shipped platinum and jumped right on the charts. People in the industry, to this day, still refer to it as 42040, its order number instead of its title.

The album took off like a rocket, so Morris brought on a new sales and marketing Guru named Ira Leslie. Ira's uncle Jerry Winston owned Morris's faithful New York/New Jersey distributor: Malverne Distribution. Because of Ira's family connections, Morris knew he could trust him with, shall we say, more intricate matters, like paying off radio stations. Morris sent Ira all over the country on a special mission. Ira would fly into Chicago, Detroit, Cleveland, St. Louis, and Houston and meet all the big powerhouse radio station reps at the gate with sealed envelopes bulging with cash. The reps would walk with him to his next flight, where Ira would say good luck and continue on. Sometimes he would fly to three or four cities in a single afternoon.

I remember sitting in Morris's office when Ira returned from one of his pay-for-play excursions. Morris barked, "Everything go okay?" Ira, who sounded almost as gruff as Morris, said, "No problems. By the way, you gave me too much money," and he threw an envelope on Morris's desk. "There's a thousand dollars left over." Morris looked at the envelope, thought for a second, and said, "You're either the smartest or the dumbest fuckin' promotion man I've ever had."

As it turned out, we ended up selling 12 million copies through the seventies. That was an awesome number. And a greatest hits album was effectively free, there were no recording costs. Morris never made that much money before.

As a follow-up to "Crystal Blue Persuasion" I recorded "Ball of Fire," which I wrote with a couple of guys from Alive N' Kickin', a band I would produce a few years later. "Ball of Fire" was a very apocalyptic kind of song and it charted very well. Morris added it to the *Greatest Hits* album as a sales tactic. He would always put one new song on a *Greatest Hits* package so you would have to buy the album to get the single. The album was the greatest-selling record Roulette ever produced.

My biggest heartache in the summer/fall of 1970 was that Red Schwartz and Morris got into their own fight over money. Red must have made Morris a millionaire fifty times over but he never made more than three hundred dollars per week. Red gave Morris an ultimatum, and Morris told him to go fuck himself. Red quit that afternoon and moved to California. It was like losing your right arm. I was miserable for weeks and kept that in my mind as my contract situation was finally reaching the boiling point. This was Morris's way. Red, George Goldner—they were all used in one way or another. Morris's original partner, Joel Kulsky, took Red's place. And Joel Kulsky's half-brother Phil Karl took over publishing. It was hard to say what anybody really did. Somewhere along the way, Kulsky ran Diamond Records, but the interworkings of these relationships are so convoluted that probably the real stories are lost forever.

Another thing that happened was that my old girlfriend from Niles named Ginger showed up in publishing one day after I got back from Hawaii. She angled a job from Phil Karl, and Ginger and I struck up the old friendship when Ronnie wasn't around. I thought I was being cool, but it was just another dagger I was putting into myself and my marriage.

CHAPTER NINE

Ball of Fire

By the end of 1969, I hadn't re-signed my contract because my lawyer, Howard Beldock, was trying to work out an arrangement to force Morris to make regular payments to me. Morris had suddenly taken a very fatherly concern over me. We seemed to be hanging out together more and more at the office, talking about business and life. It was at this time that he started inviting me up to his farm in Ghent, New York. Morris's farm was his retreat and sabbatical. I think it represented a kind of healing grace for him or at least as close to grace as Morris Levy would ever get. It was for his family and friends. It was away from New York, Roulette, the hookers, and the Mulberry Street social club. The Roulette Regulars were conspicuous by their absence. By September I was going up to his farm nearly every weekend we weren't playing out. Morris Gurlak would pick me up and we would drive up together. Other than Gurlak, I never saw any of the boys up at the farm. They came up occasionally for social functions, weddings, birthday parties, but that's all. They would have been out of their element anyway. I can't imagine them baling hay with Morris.

Clive Davis was making overtures about buying out my contract but Morris wouldn't budge. I found this out through the grapevine. The funny part was that it really never dawned on me how much I was being screwed by Morris. I had never had the money in front of me, so I never missed it in the way that I would have if, say, I had a million dollars and then next year lost a million dollars. I was making good money on the road so I always had enough to get by. Morris was so consummate in his thievery that I could never really see what was never in front of me.

The band and I spent a lot of time listening to the competition. Pete Lucia was predictably up on all the newest acts or recently released albums. The band and I had a ball listening to King Crimson, Neil Young, and Crazy Horse. It took me years to realize that *In the Court of the Crimson King* didn't come with marijuana seeds enclosed in the cover. That was our favorite rolling album, and Pete was a rolling master. Bruce Staple from Allegro competed for best dovetail joint roller with Pete. We all evolved around the same time—that is to say, our hair got longer and we got high more. I don't know if that is devolving or evolving, but we thought it was the best way to keep up with the technology, which was also evolving. Pete always managed to score the best hash, orange hash, hash laced with something or other. Bruce was sweet on Jamaican weed. For me, pot that was so good made me paranoid. I didn't like getting out of control. Being out of control scared me to death. That's why I did booze and uppers, because when you did them, even though you were out of control, you didn't think you were. I never did acid. I didn't like space drugs. I wanted something that would put you someplace.

It was a quiet time for Roulette as far as I was concerned. All Morris's partners were happy. I saw a lot of Vinnie the Chin and Tommy Ryan. The *Greatest Hits* album sold extraordinarily well through the Christmas season of 1969. For the first time, I allowed myself ever so slightly to relax and enjoy my success, and part of that was going up to Morris's farm.

We would leave on Friday and come back Sunday or Monday morning. It was great on Friday night. Morris's nonmusical friends would stop by, like Dr. Joyce Brothers and her husband. I was always amazed at the people he knew. Every once in a while something would come up that would keep him away from the farm, like attending the wedding of Bob Hope's daughter, but it would have to be something very important. The whole neighborhood was being overrun with Morris's friends like Nate, Tommy Mottola, and Vinnie the Chin's brother Father Louis Gigante. Morris had all his friends buy farms. It was about four hours from New York, between the Catskills and the Berkshires. Another thing that amazed me was that Morris's property was a working dairy farm. The house was about a hundred years old with a man-made lake bordering it on the east. There were rolling hills and huge dairy barns and a colossal blue silo with a silver top and white lettering that read "Adam Levy and Father" instead of "Morris Levy and Son." There were milking barns, and he must have had a hundred cows. Morris actually made thousands of dollars a year on milk. This was free money because the cows came with the place. He hired an independent firm to run that part of the farm. He had it down to a science. They would all be milked at this huge milk factory. They had milk machines, stalls, there was processing done on the premises, and then it was sold to the local milk company. There was a crew of people who fed the cows and mucked out the stalls. Later he expanded the farm to stables for breeding racehorses. It was eleven hundred acres. There was an entourage of locals that visited him. He was constantly buying land that touched his, constantly expanding his estate. He also had an arsenal of hunting rifles, pistols, and shotguns, and walls of ammunition. The two of us would spend hours target shooting whenever I visited.

The house was gorgeous, with a real New England feel to it,

hardwood floors, and a little breezeway in the back where Morris would chop wood for the fireplace. He had a live-in elderly couple that ran the place. She would cook in a big, expansive kitchen that always smelled like just-baked bread. There was a big parlor that Morris had turned into a game room with billiard tables and chessboards, and every room seemed to have a television. The living room had two couches and the fireplace was always roaring. It was a masterpiece. The veranda went all the way around the house. Big hallways, with about five or six bedrooms. Nome, Morris's wife, would come up Saturday morning.

Friday night, Morris and I would get loaded. Watching the fire, with our feet up, we often talked business, but I often tried to get into Morris's soul. "Let me just ask you a question. Nobody can size a deal up like you. You're like a computer on a spaceship. You can do anything. Why do you hang with these Mob guys?" He would laugh and say, "These are my friends, these are the guys I grew up with. It's what I am." That was about as honest an answer as I got out of him. Morris was in some ways a very noble character and in other ways he was a scumbag. He was a thief, and possibly a killer, and he was proud of it. But when the "noble" people in this business needed a favor, when they needed something sordid to be done, and did not want to get their hands dirty, they called Morris. Morris would love to go pitch hay, he loved manual labor, and he loved his sons and nieces and nephews. But if you crossed him, he would see you dead. He was more fun to be with than anybody. He was not lazy and he had a great sense of what was right and not right. He called it like he saw it. Who was going to tell him otherwise? The police? The government? He saw the world as a crime family, the government being the biggest thief of all. The police were corrupt. Politicians were liars and crooks. And most of the time he was right. He lived by his own morality, if you could call it that. Morris never brought up my contract during this time. He would never lower himself. He would agonize and bully my lawyer, but he never said a word to me. We were on a different level of communication.

One of the things Morris was always concerned about was me taking pills. Since we were baring our souls up at the farm, he would come back at me and say, "What do you have to take that shit for? You got more fucking talent in your little finger than the rest of these guys got in their whole bodies. You don't need that shit. If I thought that shit would do any good, I'd give all my fucking writers pills." He brought this up fairly often and I never had a good answer. I used pills more than I liked them. I used them to stay up at night because I had to get things done. I'd use them to go on stage because I'd always had a nagging dose of stage fright ever since I was a kid. Once I was onstage performing, I was fine, but that second just before you're introduced, waiting in the wings, can be terrifying. I'd use pills to write because they gave me a zany feeling that I felt I could channel into something creative. I used them to find a magic topic to write about, but I usually would then forget about it by the next day. I lost a lot of songs that way, forgetting what I had written. I never confessed this to Morris. You never wanted to expose any weakness you might have in front of Morris because he would use it against you if he needed to.

But as long as I was having hits, I knew I could always count on Morris for anything (except getting paid). As long as I was important to Morris, I always had the feeling he would be there for me. Once during one of our southern tours, a group of hillbilly promoters refused to pay us. They just said, "We all lost money ourselves, son. You don't expect us to take all the pain, do you now?" I called Morris, and he asked me if I wanted Nate to go down and talk to them. I thought about it and could not do it. Nate would have killed them with his bare hands and then enjoyed a cigarette afterward as if he'd just had sex. I told Morris no and he said, "It's your call." Another time we were playing New Jersey and the promoter again refused to pay us. When I went into his office, he had a gun on the desk. He said, "One of our guys just got out of prison and he needs money. You got a problem with that?" I asked to use the phone and called my agent. I said, "Could you tell Morris we have a problem in Red Bank." My agent kept hissing at me through the phone, "Get the hell out of there." But I was too high to care. "Just tell Morris I need him to call me." When I hung up, the promoter said, "Is that Morris Levy you're talking about?" I said, "Yeah." He reached into his pocket and pulled out a wad of hundred-dollar bills and counted out my fee. "No hard feelings," he said.

I went up to Ghent dozens of times, until Morris finally had his real estate agent, Serge Bervy, find me a place in Rensselaer County, which was one county over from Ghent, in Stephentown, New York, about twenty-six miles from Albany and eleven miles south of Pittsfield, Massachusetts. The driveway was two miles long up on top of Round Mountain. I had water rights for 31,000 acres. There were 375 acres that the immediate house and land were on and another 1,000 acres that was up on the mountain. I owned 13,000 acres in all, and it was magnificent. It was built by one of the Rockefeller sisters and her husband and never finished. Production stopped because the marriage ended. It was a big two-level house made of rosewood. After I sold it, years later, it was turned into a ski resort. We had a caretaker who looked after things because I could come up only on weekends. Morris negotiated the deal for me. Morris even covered the down payment. Of course he paid for it with my money, but it's the thought that counts. There was a mortgage that I covered. It was the biggest house I would ever live in. I started to bring my friends up for the weekend, and kept the house until 1974. The Shondells and I used to practice there. We came up on weekends and stopped at the little general store at the foot of the mountain. We would buy the place out of food, booze, and ammunition and we would just hang until Monday or Tuesday of the next week. We would drive up in the winter to purposely get snowed in.

Morris took me to the Mets game during the World Series. He got us all great tickets behind home plate. Morris wanted to pick us up in a limo, but Pete Lucia loved taking the subway. Morris was friends with Lionel Hampton, who was a great Mets fan, and the two of them went to every home game. Morris was in such a good mood. He even invited Bo and Ritchie and they both came. Morris and Lionel sat right behind them. We saw all the incredible catches by Tommy Agee.

By the end of the year, Morris finally agreed to a deal with Howard Beldock and I re-signed with Roulette. It was a ten-year contract and Morris would pay a certain amount every week against the royalty number and agreed to give me statements quarterly. This went on for a little less than a year until, one day, he simply abandoned the agreement. "Fuck you," he said, "what are you going to do about it?" And it was back to business as usual. I should have known better, and I did know better, but by this time leaving Roulette would have been like turning myself into an orphan. I just couldn't bring myself to do it and I wanted to believe that things between Morris and me had changed.

We released "She" that year, another hit for us. Jimmy Wisner in the interim had been gobbled up by Clive Davis and became head of A&R at Columbia, and he produced people like Robert

Goulet, Barbra Streisand, and Tony Bennett, but he still found time to work with me and did an incredible arrangement on "She" that included horns, strings, and a choir. It sold a lot. It wasn't as big as the last two singles but it netted us another gold record.

We started work on a brand-new concept album called *Travelin'*. It was intended to be the grittiest album we'd ever done. We wanted it not to sound like a studio album and we succeeded. It was hard guitars and drums. It was our first since *Cellophane*. Once you start down the road to concept albums, you have to keep going and keep putting yourself in different situations. This album was expensive to make right down to the cover, an original painting by Ron Lesser, who was Norman Rockwell's protégé. The painting was the band in a stagecoach with me driving the team and Morris Levy as a bandit racing after us.

Travelin' went right out on the charts in the spring of 1970. We rehearsed a new thematic show to go with the album, our first album-tour package. Our concerts had always involved playing the hit singles we had done or were currently promoting. We never did a *Crimson and Clover* album tour per se. *Travelin'* was a performance breakthrough. We costumed ourselves like on the album and combined the new set with the old hits, but it was a very different experience. Meanwhile, I was reaching the breaking point. I was accepting too many dates and popping too many pills in order to have the energy to fulfill them. One night in Birmingham, Alabama, as soon as I got off stage, I fainted. I was weak and dehydrated, and I overheard the backstage doctor say, "He looks dead." The newspapers picked that up, and when I went up to Roulette the following Monday, everybody was actually shocked that I was still alive, although Ronnie and Morris knew I was okay because I had talked to them that night.

I needed some time off. My doctor told me I had to take a rest. We had been on this hell of a ride continuously since 1966, and my voice was being destroyed from overwork and dissipation. I weighed 140 pounds; I was weak. If I wasn't in the studio I was writing. If I wasn't writing, I was performing. I had to step off the merry-go-round. Up in my agent's office, the band and I decided to take some time off. The guys wanted to take a different direction and started an act called Hog Heaven with a southern rock, contemporary Christian feel to it. They got Morris to sign them and they did an album. They had a chart single called "If It Feels Good Do It." No one intended it to be forever, but while the Shondells were working on Hog Heaven, I got the bug to go into the studio again.

My new agent, Mark Allen, was convinced that I was a great producer and thought I should loan myself out to other record companies. I started by producing Alive N' Kickin'. I had brought my old friend Bob King up in 1969. Bob and I used to play together back in South Bend and we became writing partners. He wrote most of the *Travelin'* album with me. Our writing tended to be more down to earth. We wrote a song called "Tighter Tighter" up at my farm but never did anything with it. Finally, by 1970, King and I went into the studio to cut a track with Jimmy Wisner, but I didn't like the way I sounded. That's when the idea came up to give the song to Alive N' Kickin'.

I rewrote it as a duet because the band had boy-girl leads with lots of great harmonies. We laid their vocals over my track and they sounded great. We put on their guitar and organ player and it rocked. Bob and I were very proud of it. I took it up to Morris, who flipped. Alive N' Kickin' was the only act of any consequence he signed while I was at Roulette. This was my first production outside of the Shondells, and it was a big feather in my cap. Morris even induced Red Schwartz to come back and work the single. "Tighter Tighter" became a number one record. Mark Allen suggested I produce other acts, and he gave me a band he was representing called Exile, who did another song by me and Bob King called "Church Street Soul Revival." Mark put me in touch with Clive Davis, who was head of A&R at Columbia, and that's where we recorded it. Clive loved it, and asked me to come on as a full-time producer at Columbia. Morris said nothing but I knew he was watching me out of the corner of his eye.

I became an in-house producer at Columbia and produced quite a few acts like Patty Austin, but there were always problems with Columbia about releasing records. They had things like release schedules and things that I never had to deal with at Roulette because there was just Morris. When I first came to New York and went to Columbia to get a deal for "Hanky Panky," I had to meet with the vice president of Special Products and Creative Affairs, which was all very impressive. At Roulette, that job was handled by some guy named Murray and his title was "Hey you, c'mere." A perfect example was the work I did with Exile.

The record we made was test-marketed in Louisville, Kentucky, and it went to number one, which to me meant it would go to number one every other place. Columbia had issues. They thought it might interfere with another act they were promoting, I can't recall who, and so they buried the record. They never released it beyond Louisville and I never got a good reason, to this day, why they shelved the project. They had something else to release and releasing two records at once was too complicated for them. No one knows or at least no one told me. I thought, *On Roulette this would be a number one record.* It killed me.

Mark Allen also had a deal at Paramount, which had just

opened up in the Gulf and Western building at Columbus Circle. Billy Michelle was a very respected publisher in the business and he had come on board. Don Berkheimer, who had been with RCA, also came on board. Jeff Barry was hired as an A&R man. They had just signed Melanie, who had had big hits with Buddah, and there was a great production team. Paramount had lots of capital and gave us an entire floor. Everyone was happy. I produced a couple of acts and wanted to bring some new people in. But Paramount was having big trouble with the West Coast office, which was jealous of the East Coast and did everything they could to sabotage us. The corporate world was driving me crazy. As much as I hated not being paid, Morris was a man who got the job done.

In 1970, I was cutting back on the uppers and feeling healthier than I had in a long time, but right in the middle of this Ronnie and I split up. I was just too nutty. Too many other women, too many pills, too much insanity. It was my fault. I wasn't paying any attention to her. The life of a rock and roller, on a good day, can be near madness. And I was exacerbating things. She was a good person. And I was a flaming asshole. Since I'd stopped touring I had even less time to spend at home. The divorce was hard and grueling. It was not so much that it was contentious, but as in my first divorce, there was again the sense that, in the midst of all this wonderful success, I was a failure. I was a failure at the one part of my life I should have concentrated on most. Dr. Goldstein, my shrink, had put me on quaaludes, a new wonder drug on the market at the time. I was taking too many of them, the 714 variety, which were as big as horse pills. In fact, I was taking quaaludes and Valium as well as uppers—not a good recipe for a successful marriage. It was a horrible time. I switched lawyers again, as if that would change anything. The divorce came through without complications. I actually had my parents move from South Bend and got them an apartment next door to me. As much as I kept pushing Ronnie away from me by my insane behavior, I also knew that I was no good by myself.

Mark Allen put me together with a group called Neon, and I used them to record my first solo album. I missed the Shondells very much. Although I liked these kids a lot it just wasn't as much fun as with the Shondells. My first solo album netted me two more hits, "Come to Me" and "Ball and Chain." Although they weren't the monster hits that "Crimson" was, it was good to be back on the charts. You always have to prove yourself as a solo artist.

Bob King and I kept recording and we wrote "Draggin' the Line," another studio innovation where we recorded the track before the lyric. Bob played bass, I played guitar, and Russ Leslie from Neon played drums. We recorded a long loop but kept only sixteen bars. We had tape delay on all the instruments and we had to make sure it was running at the right speed. We had to keep it right "in the pocket" because we didn't have the ability to vary the delay. It was hard to keep the kind of tempo we wanted for very long, at least at that time. We went through a sixteen-bar stretch, keeping the verse melody and a secondary melody for the bridge. We only had another ten bars of that until it went out of sync. So we stopped it right there. We'd then make copies of all these taped loops so it would stay in that hypnotic pocket. We wanted a sustaining and memorizing rhythm.

This was a real engineering feat because we basically glued the record together. The end result was this beautifully hypnotic track that I was in love with. We put it out as a B side with our version of "Church Street Soul Revival," which I had recorded the previous year with Exile. We ended up getting more airtime with the B side than with what should have been the hit. We got so much airplay that I went back into the studio and made the B side the A side, and added horns with the same kind of tape delay. I ended up taking the whole horn section on the road. It was magic and they made the record come alive. It reminded me of the horns on the Beatles' "Got to Get You into My Life." The record broke out of Los Angeles, uncharacteristically, because L.A. didn't break anything except L.A. acts. I would soon have another number one record.

Later that year I went out to Los Angeles to do *American Bandstand* and arrived just in time for the big earthquake while "Draggin' the Line" was peaking. They had the earthquake in the morning and were still having aftershocks at night when I turned on my television at the Hyatt House to see "Draggin' the Line" as a cutout on a *Greatest Hits of 1971* album. My record, currently in the top five, was being peddled as a cutout. Morris had taken my record, our record, and in order to make a fast buck, because he would reap all the profits from a cutout, completely devalued a number one hit. I was furious. I went out to drown my sorrows. I was invited over to a friend's house, a typical L.A. pad with very little furniture and lots of hash and booze. I was pretty high already, and when I sat on the floor an aftershock hit the building, making the floor rumble and quiver. I thought, *This house isn't built too well if my rear end hitting the floor could make it shake.*

That's when I met Gloria. She was living with the couple that owned the house, and we hit it off and stayed up all night. She was tall and had long, curly dark hair that reminded me of Cher. I asked her if she wanted to fly back to New York with me and she said yes. Neither of us knew we were walking into a firestorm.

Just as we got back to New York in the summer of 1971, a

gang war broke out in New York. The Gambinos were taking over the New York Mob world and soldiers from every family were being shot and killed. The Genovese family was being hit hard. As much as I was mixed up in this world, I never felt myself a part of it. I was watching close up, but I was still the kid singing "Hanky Panky," making records. My world was music.

One day in 1971, I walked into Roulette to see Morris. Karen told me Morris wasn't there. "Well, when is he going to be back?" "He won't be back for a while," she said. "Well, then I'll see him tomorrow." "He won't be back tomorrow, Tommy." "Is he up at the farm?" "No," she said, "I think he's left the country." "What!" "Do you see all the craziness that's going on? He and Nate had to leave . . . quick." "Well, when is he coming back?" "I don't know," she said. "Joel Kulsky's running things for the time being."

The cover story was that Morris and Nate had left for Spain. There was a war going on and Morris was on the wrong side. I had never heard of Morris ever running away from anything. What was I going to do? No matter how crazy things were in my private life, in my emotional, financial, and professional life, Morris was the glue that held it all together. What was I supposed to do with Joel Kulsky? The point was, he'd vanished and no one could give me a straight answer. No one knew for sure, or at least no one was saying. Were there people after Morris who wanted him dead? It was only a few weeks before that Nate had warned me again, "Don't walk outside with me. I don't know what's going to happen."

About three days later, I got a call from my lawyer, Gerry Margolis, who was a partner in Harold Orenstein's firm. Harold was one of the biggest entertainment lawyers in the country. When I arrived at Gerry's office, I was ushered into Harold's office, though I never really had any dealings with Harold personally. Harold said, "Tommy, we, ah, think you may be in trouble." I thought they were talking about my career, some lawsuit, a tax issue. I was confused. "What do you mean?" "Well," he said, choosing his words carefully. "You know about the trouble going on in the city? With the gang violence?" "I've been following it on TV," I said. "What does that have to do with me?" "You know Morris, ah, left town, don't you?" "Yes," I said, starting to get nervous for the first time. He paused and looked right at me. "Well, Tommy, it's like this. We think some people are after Morris and, ah, well, frankly, if they can't get Morris, they're going to go after what's making Morris his money . . . and that's you."

I felt hot all of a sudden, like I was coming down with a fever. "We think you could be in real danger." Harold lowered his voice as if he was telling me a secret. "These guys aren't playing around." I didn't say anything. What could I say? Then he kind of lightened up. "Good idea to get out of town for a little while until this thing blows over." "Where?" I said. "What are you talking about?" It was like they were saying, "Tom, you look a little tired. You need a vacation."

"We represent Pete Drake, you know." I did know. Pete was the greatest pedal-steel guitar player on the planet. He was the pedal steel on George Harrison's "My Sweet Lord" and he had done work with Ringo as well. "Pete would love to work with you. We've done all the groundwork. He's in Nashville. He's expecting you."

I was just about ready to lose my mind. "Do you mean I should just pick up and go to Nashville?"

"Tonight," said Harold, "if you can manage."

I couldn't believe it. I had just released "Draggin' the Line" and it was climbing up the charts. I was working a hit record and had to leave town . . . on the lam . . . like some hoodlum on

197

the run? This was a bad dream. When I left Harold's office I kept looking over my shoulder as if someone might want to gun me down. I was too scared to be angry and too paranoid to think about anything except getting out. I went home, told Gloria to pack, and booked a flight to Nashville. I was gone by morning.

But it was true, Pete Drake wanted to work with me. I also took my writing partner, Bob King, and that afternoon Pete's brother Jack, who was dying of emphysema at the time, met us at the airport with a fleet of Cadillacs and took us down to Music City Row. The record companies down there were all in little row houses, and his record company was called Stop. It had a stop sign out front. We stayed at the Holiday Inn on Music City Row, which was actually a famous resting stop. I kept trying to follow the news back in New York. Although the day-to-day business of New York didn't trickle down into Nashville, one news item did. It wasn't too long after I left that Joe Columbo, head of the Columbo crime family, was shot twice in the head at Columbus Circle during an Italian antidefamation rally. The movie *The Godfather* was soon to be released, and Joe Columbo's antidiscrimination league was making sure that the word *mafia* would not be used in the picture.

Pete put us together with Scotty Moore and D. J. Fontana, Elvis's old guitar player and drummer. Scotty Moore had a studio called Music City Recorders, where he was the engineer. He was excellent and was as good an engineer as he was a guitar player. King Robbins on piano, D.J. on drums, Bob King on bass, Dave Kirby on guitar, Buddy Spiker on fiddle, and we had ourselves a band. D.J. and Russ Leslie would play off each other, and Buddy Harmon came as a second drummer and did overdubs. They were the A team. Rhythmically, it was great, and we had the Nashville Addition from *Hee Haw* doing background vocals, with Pete, of course, on pedal steel. It was a kick-ass band. I had never made music with people like these before. They were the greatest pickers in the world. They had a number system instead of charts. You'd play the song, and if your key was C that meant you played in "one." D was four, G was five. I never saw quicker studies. Everyone knew instinctively when to come in. It was like a different kind of dance. We knocked the album out in less than three months. It was called *My Head, My Bed & My Red Guitar*. It was my only country album.

Things had died down a little in New York, literally. There weren't that many people left to kill. I gave the new album to Joel Kulsky, who was still in charge, and he said, "So, what are you, a fuckin' cowboy now?" In the beginning, it sold about four albums and that's counting the copy my mother bought. Ironically, the album got the greatest review in *Rolling Stone* magazine I ever received. Joel had hired the legendary Juggy Gayles to do promotion and sales picked up.

Morris was still gone. He wouldn't come back for another six months and by now I had reached my darkest feelings about him. Morris had abandoned me and put me in the worst situation I had ever been in. It was literally a matter of life and death. I was afraid enough to call my parents, almost in tears. My mother said, "You come right home," but the best thing for me to do was work on the new album. I kept moving in and out of extremes. There were times when I was actually worried about Morris. Then I would say, "How could that bastard leave me like this?" I felt intense rage and then a desperate kind of fatigue. I felt like I was going out of my mind. I knew that this was the end. I couldn't take it anymore. And yet, all the while, there was one nagging question that I couldn't get out of my brain. Who had called Harold Orenstein and told him to get me out of town?

Morris's disappearance allowed me to do something I'd wanted to do for a long time. I told Aaron Schechter, my accountant, "This has got to end. I can't be held hostage anymore. Do what you have to do but get me out of this nightmare." Aaron put together a very ingenious scheme. Morris hadn't paid me for years, and there were no royalty statements available. Howard Fisher, loyal as ever, could find nothing and acted just as confused as we all were. So instead of going to the pressing plants, which were also loyal, or scared to death of Morris, he went to the printing plant where Morris got his labels made—there was only one label-making plant—and he got an honest count going back for years, almost since I'd started with Roulette. The numbers were astonishing. Morris owed me upward of forty million dollars. It was just horrendous. Even with my miserable royalty rate he owed me that much. Because everything we created and pressed had sold.

It was around this time that I met Lynda. I went out one evening with a booking agent I often worked with named John Apostle. He and his partner, Jim Hudson, took me out on the town, going from club to club to listen to some bands they were promoting. We stopped by their office later that night and I struck up a conversation with their secretary. Lynda and I didn't just hit it off, we fused. I could not take my eyes off her, and when I left that night, I could not forget her. It wasn't just her looks, her personality, her style, her sense of humor, her eyes and lips . . . it was everything. The next day we had lunch, and the following weekend, I took her up to the farm after telling Gloria I had more work to do with Bob King. The next week, I told Gloria what had happened and she left, just like that. Lynda moved in later that month.

When Nate and Morris did finally come back they had grown Fu Manchu mustaches. For all I know they had spent the last year wearing nose glasses. Apparently, the crisis was over.

Within a week, Morris threw a big party for me at the Plaza

hotel. It was the "Tommy James—Gold Record Bash." Joel Kulsky was the MC. All the industry people were there. Morris honored me by presenting me with more than a dozen gold records that he had manufactured himself using the cheapest records with the tiniest holes papered over to simulate real gold records, like the ones hanging on his walls that I had won for him. My new band played and I got to introduce my new single, which turned out to be a rock song about the Prodigal Son. By the end of the night no one was sure whether it was a Tommy James party or a "Welcome Home, Morris" party.

It wasn't long before Morris made it clear that everything was going back to normal. Aaron waited a couple of weeks and went up to talk to Morris. Why hadn't Tommy been paid? Morris gave Aaron some lame excuse as usual, and Aaron turned over his hand, which he felt was four aces. "Let me tell you something, Mr. Levy. We have a real count." And he showed Morris the purchasing orders for all the labels over the years. He even had it broken down to the promotion copies, which were a different color than the ones used for retail sales. It was indisputable and honest. Morris's face froze into a kind of rigor mortis. "You owe Tommy between thirty and forty million dollars. It's that simple and we want to get paid." Morris then turned over his royal straight flush. "You ever fuckin' use that against me, and they'll fish you out of the motherfucking river. Now get out of my office." That's all he said. Aaron realized there was nothing he could do, because he knew Morris was serious. Whatever clashes Morris had with the Mob had apparently been settled and things were indeed going back to normal, if you could call it that. Aaron had a family. It was over.

I had nowhere else to turn and no one left to turn to. I had it in my mind to talk to Morris myself, and I intended to push buttons and make something happen.

That Saturday night, July 15, 1972, I was scheduled to play the Paramount Theater in Brooklyn. The Brooklyn Paramount was one of Morris's old stomping grounds, where he first had his rock and roll shows with Alan Freed in the fifties. Morris was still doing shows there in the early sixties when he had a famous screaming match with Little Richard, which ended when he pulled Richard's wig off his head in the elevator at the back of the theater and told him if he didn't shut up, "I'll tear your fuckin' face off." Morris had made rock concerts at the Paramount legendary. It was a really special date for me.

Friday afternoon, the day before the show, I was up at Roulette. We were getting ready to release our new single, "Love Song." I heard the record playing in Morris's office and walked in. Tommy Eboli was sitting with Morris listening to the new track, and he came over to me and put his hands on my shoulders. "I love this record," he said. "I love all your records. You make nice records." Even compliments from these guys could tighten your stomach. That was just the kind of thing they would say before they shot you, but this was different. I could see he really meant it. It was just so strange because I'd never heard Tommy talk that way. As good as it was for my ego, it was totally unexpected. "Thank you," I said. "That means a lot to me. You have to sell the guys in your corner before you can sell anyone else." Then he smiled at me and said, "We're all proud of you."

The show, the next night, was a sold-out, rowdy crowd, and with me on the bill was one of my all-time favorite acts and good friends, the Grass Roots. Unexpectedly, my limo driver called the theater and said he'd been in an accident and wouldn't be able to drive me home. Rob Grill, the bass player and lead singer, volunteered to drop me off at my place in Manhattan because "The Roots" were all staying up on Fifty-seventh Street at the Holiday Inn, a few blocks from my apartment. Before we left, we all got tanked backstage. It was a beautiful summer night smack in the middle of July. They had a new convertible and all I can remember is that it was red and fast. We all packed into the car, pretty well smashed, and cruised through Brooklyn, laughing and singing. One of their records, "Sooner or Later," came on the radio and we all sang along. Two girls were walking down the street and Rob jumped up on the back of the front seat, and yelled, in his best Brooklyn accent, "Roxanne, if your mother knew it would kill her," which cracked everybody up.

At almost that very moment, just a few blocks away, Tommy Eboli was coming out of his girlfriend's apartment to get into his car, when somebody walked up to him and, at point-blank range, pumped six bullets into his head and chest.

That's how so many of these guys die: fast, brutal, and without mercy. And just a day earlier, he had his hand on my shoulder telling me how much he liked my music. It almost doesn't pay to become friends with them. I really missed him. They never did catch the guys who did it.

I found out what happened to Tommy when I went up to Roulette on Monday morning. Normally, Mondays were high-energy and loud, but this day I felt like I was walking into a funeral, everything was so quiet. Karen pulled me aside and told me what had happened to Tommy. Over the next few weeks a lot of the story leaked out. Tommy was apparently mixed up in some heroin deal with the Gambinos, which right off the bat seemed insane since it had been Carlo Gambino's coming to power that had triggered the Mob wars that had killed so many of the Genovese people. Apparently the Gambinos had put up a lot of money. But somehow the feds got wind of it, arrested everybody, and confiscated both the drugs and the cash. When the Gambinos demanded that Tommy pay the money back, he either wouldn't or couldn't, and that signed his death warrant.

There were even rumors that the Gambinos tipped off the feds themselves in order to get Tommy, which would have been the final nail in the coffin from the '71 gang wars.

Once again, things were thrown into a chaotic state at Roulette. I remember Morris really looked bad. He was visibly shaken by this. Tommy Eboli was not only Morris's connection and protection "downtown," but they had been pals for a long time. I felt like I should say something consoling to Morris, but what the hell was I going to say? And after my forced hibernation in Nashville the previous year because of Morris's Mob shit, I had really had it. One way or the other . . . I was getting the fuck out of here!

There wasn't much time for mourning before I went in to see Morris. There was never a good time to confront Morris about anything, especially money, but I did not care. I had had enough. I walked in high on uppers to keep my energy level as acute and searing as I could. It was the most upsetting thing I ever had to do. The confrontation started loud and got louder and more and more visceral. There was venom in every word we said to each other. It was like we had been rehearsing our final act for the past six years. I didn't care anymore. I was overwhelmed with pills and booze and resentment. I was sick to death of Morris Levy. Morris was behind the desk, sitting down. I did not sit down.

"Aaron told me what you said to him. I can't believe you told him that."

"Fuck your accountant. Nobody threatens me, you understand?"

"I'm so sick of this bullshit. I'm sick of you and I'm real sick of not being paid. I made you a fortune. I'm sick of living this kind of fucked-up life, living with your gangster friends and worried if somebody is going to blow my brains out because I work for you."

"You do what the fuck you're told."

"Fuck you," I screamed. "I'm one of the most successful acts on the planet and I have to beg for money like some bum off the street. I have two dozen gold records and I have to come to you with a tin cup. Jesus Christ, Morris, I even had to steal my fucking gold records off the wall. I'm sick of trying to make music for some ungrateful fuck like you. I'm getting out of here."

"You ain't going anywhere. Sit down and shut up."

"What are you going to do?" I said. "Beat my brains out like you did to Jimmie Rodgers?"

"Listen, you little prick. There wouldn't be a Tommy James if it wasn't for me."

"You're psychotic, you know that? You and your fucking obsession with other people's money."

He sounded like the possessed girl in *The Exorcist*. "You were some fucking nobody 'til I put my money into you. I made you a fucking star, you ungrateful little shit."

"Fuck you. I would have been a star without you. Every record company was going to sign me until you put a fucking gun to their heads. I'm going someplace where I'm appreciated. I don't care if you fucking shoot me. It's better than living this fucked-up life."

"I held still for all your fucking craziness. You and your fucking pills and your booze. You still owe me money from all the recording sessions."

"Oh, really. Did they cost forty million fucking dollars? You cocksucking thief."

"Fuck forty million dollars. Fuck you. Fuck Tommy James. You think you're a big man now. You ain't going nowhere." He paused and looked at me. His eyes were popping out of his head. "Don't try nothing either or you'll be sorry."

"You might as well do it now." I stood up and threw my arms out. "Come on, shoot me now, you son of a bitch. I'm leaving."

I walked out and smashed the door against the wall. No one said a word to me, not even Karen. For once, everybody up there was afraid of me instead of Morris. I don't remember ever being that angry, to the point that I didn't care what happened to me. If Morris had touched me and I had a knife I would have stabbed him like he told me he'd stabbed his brother's killer. I don't know whether I made an impression, but I know Morris had never seen me like that before.

I went home and was sick for weeks. Every time the phone rang I thought it might be him but he never called. I knew in my heart he would never call. That wasn't Morris's way. I hit him with everything I had and it did not faze him. It wasn't anything a hundred other people hadn't said to him. I stayed high for a couple of days and then concocted my plan. No matter what I said, Morris had me over a barrel. And no matter what he might have thought of me, he wasn't going to let me risk his security or jeopardize his home and family, his hookers and Mob friends, his power and authority. The only way I could beat Morris was to sabotage my own career. I could have sued him but Morris didn't care about lawsuits. Morris was a law unto himself. And when it came down to it, you weren't just fighting Morris. You were fighting all of them, the whole Genovese crime family. And they had no problem shooting their own people. What would they care about a long-haired rocker and his accountant? It was the only way out. Everything I had worked so hard to create, everything I had ever dreamed of, would have to lie in ruins by my own hand. That was the killer. I was the one who would have to destroy Tommy James. If I didn't, whatever was left of Tommy Jackson would not survive.

I decided that I would make no more albums for Roulette. Morris kept sporadically releasing whatever singles he had stored in the vault but the well soon ran dry.

In 1974, he finally let me go. I had changed lawyers again and David Carrabelle finally got me out of my contract. My publishing had to stay with Morris for several more years, but in 1974, Morris finally gave me my release. I felt terrible in one respect. This was my home. But everything had changed. There were dark clouds in the sky now. My marriage was over, Red was gone, and Morris was spending more time up at the farm. Tommy Eboli had been shot along with all the others lost in the gang wars. The ground under the music business was shifting. It seemed like everything was out of joint. The whole sense of play had gone away. Thank God I had found Lynda. She was the only thing keeping me sane.

By 1974, I was gone.

CHAPTER TEN

Draggin' the Line

Just before I officially separated from Roulette, Morris got into a curious haggle with John Lennon. The Beatles had released their album *Abbey Road* back in 1969. The first song on the album was John's song "Come Together." In the mid-seventies, Morris discovered that a couple of lines from "Come Together" were taken from a Chuck Berry song called "You Can't Catch Me," and Morris owned the copyright. The Chuck Berry song was about a car chase with a "flat-top" "moving up" on Chuck's car. There was a similar line in "Come Together." Morris and his publishing company, Big Seven, sued John Lennon and his publishing company, as well as the Beatles' record company, Apple Records. But Morris never collected on the suit, because he and John had become friends. Whether he wanted to find someone to replace me as Roulette's main money earner by trying to steal John from Capitol or whether he just wanted to be associated with an ex-Beatle, I don't know. Whatever his motives, Morris talked John into recording three songs from his publishing company for the next Lennon album, a project John was planning with Phil Spector. John was going to do a cover album of fifties rock and roll classics. Recording the three Morris songs would satisfy the suit. I found out from Karen later on that Morris had invited John down to his house in Jupiter, Florida, and offered John his farm in upstate New York for rehearsals. Morris was courting John.

Things didn't work out. John was late with the recording, and by this time Capitol Records had gotten involved. Morris not only wanted to have John record his songs, he also wanted to handle the distribution, which he intended to do through television marketing; a virgin field that Morris wanted to control. Capitol was distributing John's albums and told Morris to get out of the picture. Morris said that if Capitol didn't back down he would release his own John Lennon album of outtakes that John had foolishly loaned him and that Morris had no intention of giving back. John called Morris, almost in tears, and begged him not to release the record, but Morris, of course, said, "Fuck you."

Morris released *Roots* and Capitol hurried out what became *Rock and Roll*. But by this time, everybody was suing everybody else. The case dragged on for another year and Morris lost. None of this surprised me. Morris made millions and would go on to make more, but there was something inside him that could not do it legitimately. Morris would always rather make ten cents illegally than a thousand dollars honestly. Thank God, I thought, it wasn't my problem anymore.

Now I was on my own. My manager was still Mark Allen, and he got a deal for me at Fantasy Records. At that point, I wanted to get as far away from New York as I could, and Fantasy was out in Berkeley, California. Just before that, I did a short stint at MCA with a single that I had just recorded called "Glory Glory." We had a single on MCA, which got some airplay but didn't do that much. MCA had just opened a New York office, and George Lee from Warner Brothers came over and headed it and Carol Ross, the greatest PR gal on the planet, worked there, so it was a great place. But MCA was not going to spring for albums. They already had Elton John and Olivia Newton-John, and my name didn't end in John, so I left.

Then I went to Fantasy and released two albums: *In Touch* and *Midnight Rider*. While I was with Fantasy, I had to finagle a deal with Jeff Barry because Morris would not give up my publishing. Anything I wrote up to 1979 was his. Anything that had my name on it, even though it had Jeff Barry's name attached to it, would go through Morris and he would claim rights, which would mean that Jeff would never get paid either. So Jeff, knowing this, asked me if every other song on *Midnight Rider* could be a Tommy James song and he would claim credit for the other half, and that's what we did.

I had gone up to see Morris at one point. The album was starting to go up the charts, and I made a point of stopping by Roulette while I was in New York just to say hello, but I really wanted to stick it to him. I was high, but not like at our last meeting. I was filled not so much with anger as I was full of myself. We were meeting for the first time as equals, at least in my mind. I almost said, "You have my publishing? Fine. Let's see you get out of this." After some pleasantries and talk about the good old days, I left him a copy of the album and walked out.

Morris went crazy. He called Jeff Barry and scared Jeff to death. "I know what you guys are trying to pull. This is bullshit. You think I don't know a Tommy James song when I hear it?" Jeff called me and screamed, "Why did you go see Morris, for Christ's sake? You trying to get me killed?" But Morris could not prove anything. I wanted to stick a pole into the lion's cage and rattle it and make him roar.

While I was out in California, I visited Red Schwartz, who had married and relocated to the West Coast, as far away from

Morris as possible. We had lunch at an L.A. restaurant and talked old times. When I mentioned Nate McCalla, Red said, "Didn't you hear?" I said, "Hear what?" Red got nervous and spoke softly, like he used to do at Roulette when the boys were in Morris's office. "They found Nate's body in a bungalow in Florida. He was strapped to a chair and had been shot in the face. The body must have been there for a couple of weeks." We traded stories about what we had heard of Nate since we'd both left Roulette, that he was running guns, that he owed the wrong people money and had to leave the country but he couldn't stay away. Knowing Nate, both stories were probably true. The funny thing was that all the time we were talking, no matter how insane the situation was, how insane the world of Morris Levy was, we realized it still had been the best time of our lives.

I signed eventually with Millennium Records back in New York, which produced the *Three Times in Love* album and the single of the same name. It was a successful album and the single went number one, plus two other chart singles, "You Got Me" and "You're So Easy to Love." I then left Millennium and signed with Freddie Hyan, the president of Polygram, who had started his own label called 21 Records. We were right in the middle of doing an album when he lost his distribution deal with Polygram, and because of another problem he had over taxes, and because he was a Dutch citizen, had to leave the country at the request of the federal government.

On April 17, 1981, Lynda and I were married in a little church her parents attended in Mars, Pennsylvania, just outside Pittsburgh. Lynda was a Pittsburgh girl. I was very happy and content that once again the town of Pittsburgh had changed my life. You would think that after everything I had been through, I would learn a lesson, any lesson. Not likely. In 1986, I got high and decided to see Morris Levy.

I had written some new songs and recorded them as rough mixes. I do not know what compelled me except that I wanted him to see what I had done on my own. I wanted his approval. As insane as it was, I missed Roulette and the electricity of the place. I missed the sixties. I went up to Morris's new offices on Broadway. The space was big but it wasn't nice. It had all the outward things that Roulette always had, but none of the people that I had grown up with, none of the people that made it work. Morris's office was strangely the same. The same plaques, the picture of Cardinal Spellman, the UJA awards, and the great desk. Morris was making his usual fortune. He was involved in a lot of cutout deals. He had bought Strawberries, which was a huge record store chain out of Boston, and he went all over the country building outlets. Morris, of course, loved the new stuff. "This is a fuckin' hit." I told him I wasn't looking for a record deal. "I want my own label," I told him. "You got it." No hesitation. We drew up papers. The lawyers got together, but in the end I could not sign. I could not do it. One of the points of the deal was that I could not collect my own money. It would all have to go through Roulette. There was no way I could do it. Morris would just keep the money.

Morris was very glad to see me. He had not had a hit to speak of since I left. He was making his money from his catalog, Strawberries, and his cutouts and marketing deals with his new companies, Adam VIII and K-tel.

About three months later, I was watching the news about an MCA/FBI sting. My mouth dropped open. Brian Ross on NBC News was announcing, "Morris Levy, the Godfather of rock and roll, has just been arrested at his Boston offices." They had shots of the MCA building in Hollywood. Morris was arrested at one of his Strawberries stores and taken out in handcuffs. He had a suit coat over his cuffs. The FBI must have cued the TV stations.

At first I was stunned. Seeing Morris arrested and in handcuffs was as upsetting as if I had seen my parents arrested. I thought it was impossible. Morris beating the rap, any rap, was almost a law of nature to anyone who knew him. The thought of him going to prison was as inconceivable and chaotic as if the laws of gravity had been turned upside down. But as I followed the story more closely and talked to people who were still close to Morris, I became furious. The feds had Morris's office staked out for months. There were microphones under the desk, embedded in the walls, cameras spying on all proceedings from two discreet holes drilled into the ceiling. One directional microphone was behind the O on his favorite plaque, "O Lord, Give Me a Bastard with Talent." And the mikes and the cameras were running when I had gone up to see Morris. Now I likely had my own separate file in FBI headquarters. I kept trying to remember every word I'd said. Did I say anything incriminating? Was I going to be considered one of Morris's partners? Was my home in New Jersey bugged? Did the FBI sneak in while Lynda and I were away? I was seething and scared and still in amazement over Morris's arrest. I had tried to escape Morris, and yet I came back. No one forced me to go up to Morris. There was a part of me that missed the insanity, excitement, power, glamour, and danger of it all.

That night I went home and started drinking heavily. Lynda was sympathetic, but as soon as I went over the edge, she went to bed in disgust. At some point during the night I began taking out what was left of my gun collection, the one that Morris took from me years before and kept at his farm. I eventually got most of them back and kept them up at my farm, but when that was sold I brought them to New Jersey. I don't know whether I was paranoid about the FBI or if the guns brought Morris back to me in a kind of drunken reverie. It's always pointless to speculate why a drunk does what he does, because all the reasons are hidden inside a bottle and they make sense only to the one doing the drinking. Apparently, at some point, I loaded up one of my rifles, opened the kitchen window, and started firing the thing at my pool in the backyard. One, two, three, I don't remember how many times, I don't remember what I hit, what I was aiming at. The next thing I remember was the police at my door.

Lynda was frantic. I was calm, reserved even, most likely in that comatose state of awe when the lights go up and you just don't care anymore. My whole gun collection was scattered over the living room floor. One of my neighbors had heard the shots and called the police. It wasn't long before I was led out of my house in handcuffs. The police gathered all my weapons as evidence and I was driven to the station, where I spent the night in jail.

When I woke up the next morning I was terrified and in a state of panic. I had no idea what I had done. Did I take the car out and kill somebody? Did I hurt Lynda? Those initial seconds of dread were the most frightening I had ever known. What had I done? I could not remember.

Lynda eventually bailed me out and called my attorney, but no attorney I had ever had was going to help me with this mess. When everything had been explained to me, all I could think about was Morris. Why didn't I listen to Morris and get rid of those guns? He was right and I was crazy. For a second I actually thought about calling him, asking him for help. Morris, get me out of this. But Morris could not do that anymore. There were no more adults left to call. And why should there be? I was almost forty years old. My lawyers worked feverishly on my case, I prayed like I had never prayed before, and, by some miracle, I was found guilty of nothing more than disturbing the peace. I knew, in my heart, that God was giving me one last chance.

It was right after that that I decided I had to do something drastic. I initially was going to go to England for a radical treatment that was popular back then. I was desperate enough to do anything. Then I saw Liza Minnelli on *60 Minutes*. Liza had just come out of Betty Ford and she raved about the place and I decided to go, but I could not go right away. We had a lot of concerts already booked and we would have been sued for a lot of money if I did not keep the dates. The last day I got high was October 9, 1986, in Atlantic City, when I really tied one on at the gambling tables. I won a lot of money too. Lynda went with me out to the Ford Center on the thirteenth. We flew into Palm Springs, and they picked me up and took me to the center. Lynda was going to stay with friends while I was getting treatment, and it was six of the best weeks I ever spent in my life. I haven't had a drink or mind-altering chemical since. It changed my whole life. One of the most dramatic moments for me was the realization that I was a Christian who did everything a Christian should not do. I could no longer live with that hypocrisy and double-mindedness. When you're cross-addicted as I was, you have no real conception of how saturated you are with that poison. As it wears off, a weird thing starts to happen. Your feelings come back to life. It's like you are watching black-and-white TV and someone switches on the color. I wanted to laugh and cry at the same time. I had not felt this good or healthy in thirty years. I did not realize I was a flat-liner. My world had become colorless, and now I could see it in all its splendor. I felt like I had been in a coma or under anesthesia for the last two decades and now I was waking up. I couldn't wait to do all the things I had erased from my life, simple things like going to the movies, taking walks, looking at the ocean, living.

This gush of emotions even worked itself into my songwriting. I actually started using verbs again. I gained almost an octave in my voice. It was like being born again. It was truly a death, burial, and resurrection. I left my old corpse back at the center and walked out a new person.

I tried for about three weeks, but I couldn't read, and the only book I brought with me was my Bible. All your muscles are contracting when you've been on Valium. You look at something and the writing flies off the pages and escapes before you can comprehend. When my eyes refocused I said, "Lord, I'm going to open a page of the Bible and I want you to guide my hand. Please stop me where you want me to read." I opened to Psalm 32, a conversation between David and God.

> Be ye not as the horse, or as the mule, which have no understanding.

I could not believe it, but it just seemed like God talking to me. Really talking to me. I showed it to my roommate, who was younger than I was. He read the passage and tears came to his eyes too.

> I will guide thee with mine eye.

It was God talking to me and giving me this great chance to be a new man, a new husband and father, even a new musician.

> Thou art my hiding place; Thou shalt preserve me from trouble; Thou shalt compass me about with songs of deliverance.

I got out of the Ford Center right around the anniversary of the Kennedy assassination, on November 22, 1986. We stayed with friends in Palm Springs, and I relished the freedom and sheer pleasure of it all. It was brand new to me. I was brand new to me. We leased a place from Barry Manilow. Lynda and I stayed there for several months and adapted pretty well to the California lifestyle. It was also great to be near the Ford Center, just in case. We picked fruit for our breakfast from trees in our backyard and sat in the spa all afternoon. I was being reeducated about life, a life I had missed, a life that wasn't locked away in a studio, or dressing room, or a cramped office at Roulette. But the best part was finally being able to practice what I had for so long preached but could never really fathom. I was finally living like a Christian, or at least the best Christian I could be, rather than all the double-talk, the double-mindedness that had so absorbed me and kept me so fundamentally, essentially unhappy.

Howie Silverman and David Fishoff came out to see me and asked if they could manage me. I said yes. David at that time was managing the entire front line of the New York football Giants, who were headed to the Super Bowl that year. He invited me to go. Howie Silverman is still my agent. This was also part of growing up and living without booze and pills. People were no longer expendable and replaceable. They were people.

I went back home to New Jersey. It was weird getting used to my house again. I got a call from Pete Lucia, my old drummer from the Shondells, who had just gotten a job in the A&R department at Capitol Records in L.A. He asked me if I would consider producing some groups for Capitol. I said yes. My whole life right then was just saying yes. We were going to get together when I came out to the Super Bowl. Lynda and I went into the city that week and met with Phil Simms, McConkey, Bavaro, and all the rest of the team at the Hard Rock Café. There was a big press party, and I sat at the head table and was elected as the sort of unofficial mascot for the team. That night, January 6, I got a call from Pete's sister that Pete had just died. He had a heart murmur for years that we all knew about and it finally took its toll. One month before his fortieth birthday he was playing golf and had just finished the front nine. He went into the clubhouse and collapsed. He was dead before he hit the ground. The medic tried for over an hour but he was gone. I called all the Shondells and we got together for the first time since our unintended breakup, and went to Pete's funeral in New Jersey. I called Morris, and he was very saddened by Pete's death. I think he must have felt that was the beginning of the end of so many things. He told me that if Pete's family needed anything, to let him know. Anything at all. And I believe he meant it deeply.

I finally returned to the road. It was a great concert year and I was able to take more dates than I ever did before. At the Betty Ford Center they all told me to take it easy in the beginning, take it slow; be careful and start out with small venues until you get your nerves back. I had confessed, at the center, to always having stage fright and needing to get half-lit before I went on. Howie booked my first date back at Madison Square Garden. So much for small venues. I got on stage and my legs were shaking. The first song we did was "Draggin' the Line" and I forgot the words, but after three songs into the set I was having a ball. I wasn't acting anymore. I realized that for years I had been scripting and choreographing every move I ever made: at this point . . . smile; at this point . . . take small bow. I was like a programmed robot. But at that Garden show I was completely spontaneous. If I felt like screaming, I screamed. If I felt like kicking my leg, I did. And the audience could sense it. They were giving back to me in a way I hadn't felt since those early days playing the surf clubs up and down Lake Michigan when I was a kid with the Tornadoes. I was really free and I regained an incredible sense of "now." If I did something, the reaction was *now*. I was in the groove. I couldn't wait to do the next show. But more profoundly, I knew that if I stayed sober and kept to my program; if I did good work or at least the best work I could do; the Lord would move heaven and earth to bless me.

Morris was set for trial in 1987. It took his lawyers months to read the roomful of transcriptions the FBI had amassed. Morris was involved in more scams than anyone ever realized or could document. But the cutout business was his Stradivarius and he played it like a virtuoso.

Morris had a record company called Promo Records that he had owned with Tommy Eboli, and through that label, Morris effectively invented the cutout business. He created companies like Adam VIII or partnered with companies like K-tel to push through television promotions whatever albums he had overstocked. Usually he would put compilation albums together filled with songs to which he owned the publishing rights. But more insidiously, he concocted an even better scam.

Morris knew that if you created a second label as an adjunct to your main label and pressed records that never sold, you could write off your expenses to the IRS. Morris had dozens of labels under the Roulette umbrella. Some were legitimate labels that usually defined a specific genre, like rock, doo-wop, jazz, folk, comedy, Latin, or the latest flavor of the month. But some, like the Tiger Lily label, were nothing more than tax scams. Morris used Tiger Lily like a garage sale. He took random recordings that had been accumulating in his vaults and pressed them up under the Tiger Lily label and then warehoused them. They were never actually sent out to retailers. If they were sent out, it was only in tiny shipments meant to give the impression of vast distribution. Some of the material was by legitimate artists but most of the albums pressed were from kids who had sent crudely made tapes of their songs to Roulette on the million-to-one shot of hitting the big time. Very rarely was there a recognizable name on the cover. Everything had plausible deniability and there were one or two legitimate sales receipts to shut up nosy investigators asking questions. Most of the obscure bands on Tiger Lily had no idea an album of their material was even made. Morris would press up a few hundred copies of each album, claim he'd actually pressed up 25,000 or more, and then claim the loss. Other record companies followed Morris's lead. Most of the records were held in secret warehouses for a couple of years and then dumped or slowly fed to backwater retailers who handled that kind of thing. By the time Morris owned his record store chain, Strawberries, he was making money on the venture three ways. But it also became his downfall.

Music Corporation of America was an entertainment giant out of Chicago that ran nightclubs, record labels, and artists, and managed entertainers as big as Bob Hope, Johnny Carson, and Ronald Reagan. MCA always played both ends against the middle. Their Mob ties went back to the Al Capone days. They tried to cover themselves politically by being the largest contributor to the Reagan Presidential Library, to the tune of half a million dollars. In 1984, MCA wanted to sell about five million cutouts for a little over a million dollars. A retailer out of Pennsylvania named John LaMonte was designated to accept shipment, which proved to be a convoy of about sixty eighteen-wheelers. There were some first-class albums involved in the deal, by artists like Elton John, the Who, and other top acts. Everyone involved in the intermediate transactions were mobsters or wannabes. The FBI got involved because they were investigating MCA, mostly for tax evasion. The transaction was handled by Morris Levy and his associate Sonny Vastola. Morris saw a way to make a quick killing, and before the shipment arrived at LaMonte's warehouse, the boys had skimmed the shipment of all the most salable records. When LaMonte took possession and checked the inventory, he realized he was being cheated and refused to pay the bill. That is when things fell apart.

Because LaMonte had a conviction for counterfeiting (record albums, of course), the FBI became interested when his name came up in connection with MCA. They broke into the Roulette offices in the middle of the night and placed microphones and video cameras in Morris's inner sanctum. They watched and listened. For over a year, Morris and Sonny tried everything they could to get LaMonte to pay but he would not budge. They brought in Mob negotiators to try to mediate the problem. They threatened to take over LaMonte's business. Sonny and some of his associates personally went to Pennsylvania to persuade LaMonte, but they could do nothing except put him in the hospital for six weeks while doctors reconstructed his face with wire. After that, LaMonte agreed to wear another kind of wire, and the feds eventually had a case against Morris for racketeering and extortion.

I, on the other hand, was doing pretty well. I was touring and spending winters in Palm Springs. Sometime in the summer of 1987, Billy Idol put out a cover of "Mony Mony" and Tiffany did her version of "I Think We're Alone Now." Neither knew the other was doing a Tommy James song. On a flight out to a date, Lynda put a copy of *Billboard* in front of me. Both artists were reviewed the same week and both were going up the charts like they were holding hands. By October, both records went number one. The first time cover versions of an artist's hits had gone back-to-back number one. We were getting a lot of covers of our songs by then and a lot of movies were using our songs as part of their soundtracks. In a real howler, ICM was putting a movie deal together about Jerry Lee Lewis called *Great Balls of Fire* starring Dennis Quaid, and they offered me the role of Jimmy Swaggart. I wisely and respectfully declined. It is always the thought that counts.

I went to the Super Bowl at the Rose Bowl and the Giants won. I went back to the Betty Ford Center and talked to some of the new patients. Red was out in California by now selling cars, and whenever I was in L.A. I would call him and we would meet for dinner. I was with Red when we got the word that Morris had been convicted. Joel Diamond, a friend of mine and a music publisher, told us over lunch. No one expected this. It seemed inconceivable that Morris could get caught at anything. He was given a ten-year sentence, which we knew he would beat on appeal. He had to beat it. He was Morris. The feeling was, put him up before a firing squad, but in an orange jumpsuit? Never.

As soon as the conviction went through, Morris began selling off his holdings. He sold everything except the farm in Ghent. He sold Roulette to Rhino Records, which was then distributed by EMI. Big Seven Publishing was sold to Windswept Pacific, which was owned by Chuck Kaye and a Japanese company called JVC. Strawberries was bought by a company owned by Jose Menendez. When Menendez and his wife were murdered, the FBI came to Morris. "What the fuck am I going to kill the guy for, you assholes? He just wrote me a check for forty-seven million dollars." As it turned out, the Menendez children actually killed their parents. The point was that suddenly all of my music was out on CD. For the first time in my career I was getting paid royalties, and the checks were mind-boggling, in some cases six and even seven figures per year. My music was being represented intelligently and fairly all over the world. Our concert price went up and I was even getting foreign residuals, not to mention radio airplay. Britain started playing my records again. Life was good.

I knew about Morris in late 1989, that he had been diagnosed with cancer, and that it wasn't good. I knew that he had lost his appeal but that the sentence had been commuted because he was so sick, but even then, I could not bring myself to believe that Morris was going to die. He tried to emigrate to Australia, for some reason, and wanted to take all his friends with him, but the Australian government had done its homework and denied him entry. The end was coming. All his old cronies— those who were still alive, anyway—ex-employees like Karen, his ex-wives, children, nieces and nephews, old Roulette artists all made the pilgrimage to the farm to say their goodbyes. According to Karen, Little Richard called every day trying to get Morris to pray with him. Morris weakly, politely, declined. He lay in bed mostly and smoked pot to ease the pain of the cancer. He seemed happy and resigned.

I don't know why I didn't call. I thought, "I don't have to believe this if I don't want to." I should have gone up to see him. I should have canceled this damned concert. How many times had I said that in my life to my wives, my son, and now to Morris?

The interviewer looked at me. "Mr. James, I've run out of cassettes." I looked at him for a second as if he were crazy. "How long have I been talking?" "A while," he said. "Everybody's gone." He was right. The band, my wife, Carol, Ron had all gone back to the hotel. Finally, the DJ packed up his tape recorder and left too. The last thing he said to me was "I'm sorry . . . about Morris."

I put on my jacket, grabbed my guitar, and walked down the

long corridor to the stage door. I opened it up and went outside and there was the limo. The air was cool and the sky was bright with stars. The rear door of the limo was already open and I got inside. As I shut the door, I turned to my left and I swear I could almost see Morris sitting there taking a puff from his Pall Mall, blowing out the smoke, and the starlight from the window coming through the smoke. "Still on that ride, huh? You're doing good, kid." I said, "I knew they'd never get you," and he just laughed as we took off together into the night.

ACKNOWLEDGMENTS

The authors would like to thank the following men and women for their help and remembrances: Paul Colby, Carmine De Noia, Karen Grasso, Eddie Gray, Lynda James, Normand Kurtz, Ira Leslie, Zak Levy, Herbie Rosen, Ronnie Rosman, Red Schwartz, Mike Vale, and Jimmy Wisner. Special thanks to Tommy's personal manager, Carol Ross Durborow, without whom this book would never have happened. Special thanks to Ed Osborne for his editorial work and Mark Singer for his archival research. A very special thanks to our agents, Bob Levine and Kim Schefler, for their hard work and faith in this project and to everyone at Scribner and Simon & Schuster, especially Brian Belfiglio, Aisha Cloud, vice president and editor in chief Nan Graham, senior editor extraordinaire Brant Rumble, and the tireless Anna deVries.